TRIBAL DANCES OF INDIA

TRIBAL DANCES OF INDIA

USHA MEHTA

CYBER TECH PUBLICATIONS
4264/3, Ansari Road, Daryaganj, New Delhi-110002 (India)
Ph.: 011-23244078, 011-43559448 Fax: 011-23280028
E-Mail: cyberpublicationsdelhi@yahoo.com
Website: www.cybertechpublications.com

TRIBAL DANCES OF INDIA

USHA MEHTA

First Edition 2011

Published by :

G.S. Rawat for Cyber Tech Publications
4264/3, Ansari Road, Daryaganj, New Delhi-110002 (India)
Ph.: 011-23244078, 011-43559448 Fax: 011-23280028
E-Mail: cyberpublicationsdelhi@yahoo.com
Website: www.cybertechpublications.com

CONTENTS

Contents

The tribal dances in India are inimitable examples of communities in inaccessible existence, still upholding their life, customs and manners. Though adapted to different dialects and customs, the dances‘ aesthetic expression manifestly reflects the distinct, isolated and primitive social structure and nature of the people. Such tribal dances still survive in as much vigorous manner as ever in the tribal hamlets of the hilly tracts. Each of these aboriginal tribes possesses its own distinguishable dance traditions and invariably all of them are interwoven with the life of the people who dance it.

In some instances of Indian tribal dances, the dancing is awfully simple and comprises little more than insignificant mixing of the feet or waving of the hands. At other times it is just swaying of the body to the clapping of hands, or beating of primitive drums to designate time. Yet another tribal dance form demonstrates only the monotonous movement of the hands and feet. But, generally speaking, a wide range of movement requiring all parts of the body, the head, back, hips, arms, fingers and the feet and even facial muscles are employed in tribal dances.

Tribal dances are performed strictly by India‘s aboriginal populations. These people, sometimes denominated as adivasi, possess a culture, distinct from the pan Indian population. It may be noted here that Indian tribal dances are vastly dissimilar from Indian folk dances, which can never be related. A common example of a tribal dance is the Santhali dance, indigenous from West Bengal. Other tribal dances of India include the Dhimsa dance by Oriya tribes, the Dhimsa dance, yet another tribal dance from Andhra Pradesh, the Nagaland tribal dances. There exist extremely complicated Indian tribal dances as well, in which dancing melds with gesture, evincing the whole spectrum of sentiment. In such instances, the rhythm is maintained by swaying the body and intricate steps executed with expert foot-work. Usually the dances begin in a slow note, gathering momentum in the middle and working up to a heavy tempo. Which is excellently employed with enthusiastic climax of the drums and the ecstasy of the escalading rhythm of spontaneous music? Many of these tribal dances are heroic or martial in character.

Some Indian tribes pen down their songs themselves to accompany their dances. Either the dancers sing themselves or the onlookers sing and participate. Special musical instruments for Indian tribal dances are also utilised at times, but the drum is almost a requisite feature.

—Author

1

Introduction

Tribal dances are performed strictly by India's aboriginal populations. These people, sometimes denominated as adivasi, possess a culture, distinct from the pan Indian population. It may be noted here that Indian tribal dances are vastly dissimilar from Indian folk dances, which can never be related. A common example of a tribal dance is the Santhali dance, indigenous from West Bengal. Other tribal dances of India include the Dhimsa dance by Oriya tribes, the Dhimsa dance, yet another tribal dance from Andhra Pradesh, the Nagaland tribal dances.

The tribal dances in India are inimitable examples of communities in inaccessible existence, still upholding their life, customs and manners. Though adapted to different dialects and customs, the dances' aesthetic expression manifestly reflects the distinct, isolated and primitive social structure and nature of the people. Such tribal dances still survive in as much vigorous manner as ever in the tribal hamlets of the hilly tracts. Each of these aboriginal tribes possesses its own distinguishable dance traditions and invariably all of them are interwoven with the life of the people who dance it.

In some instances of Indian tribal dances, the dancing is awfully simple and comprises little more than insignificant mixing of the feet or waving of the hands. At other times it is just swaying of the body to the clapping of hands, or beating of primitive drums to designate time. Yet another tribal dance form demonstrates only the monotonous movement of the hands and feet. But, generally speaking, a wide range of movement requiring all parts of the body, the head, back, hips, arms, fingers and the feet and even facial muscles are employed in tribal dances.

There exist extremely complicated Indian tribal dances as well, in which dancing melds with gesture, evincing the whole spectrum of sentiment. In such instances, the rhythm is maintained by swaying the body and intricate steps executed with expert foot-work. Usually the dances begin in a slow note, gathering momentum in the middle and working up to a heavy tempo. Which is excellently employed with enthusiastic climax of the drums and the ecstasy of the escalading rhythm of spontaneous music? Many of these tribal dances are heroic or martial in character.

Some Indian tribes pen down their songs themselves to accompany their dances. Either the dancers sing themselves or the onlookers sing and participate. Special musical instruments for Indian tribal dances are also utilised at times, but the drum is almost a requisite feature.

Costumes of the dancers vary from estimated bareness

to full attire and ornaments which are exceedingly colourful and ornate. Tribal people make up an indispensable segment of the teeming millions in the country. India owns the second largest tribal sects in Kerala. Paniya, Adiya, Urali, Kattunaikka, Irula, Muduva, Aranadan are the high-flying tribal communities. Some of the more well known tribal dances of Kerala include Elelakkaradi, Kadarkali, Kurumbarkali, Paniyarkali, Edayarkali, Mudiyattam and Vedarkali.

Besides Kerala, India is dotted with tribal dances, surviving strong in different parts of the states and union territories. The remarkable Indian tribal dance "Brato" of Bengal, is essentially an invocational dance, preferred by barren women, worshipping their presiding deity after entreaties for progeny is answered. The legendary "Bihu" dance of Assam is part of the Bihu Utsav after the harvest season is over. Both men and women perform it in daylight. For Bihu, the dancers sing and structure themselves in parallel rows or circles. Drums and pipes accompany the dance and music. The Nagas from Nagaland have their own harvest dance "Khambahim". It is a variety performed by two separate groups of men and women, each standing in a separate row. "Akhu" is another similar Indian tribal dance form.

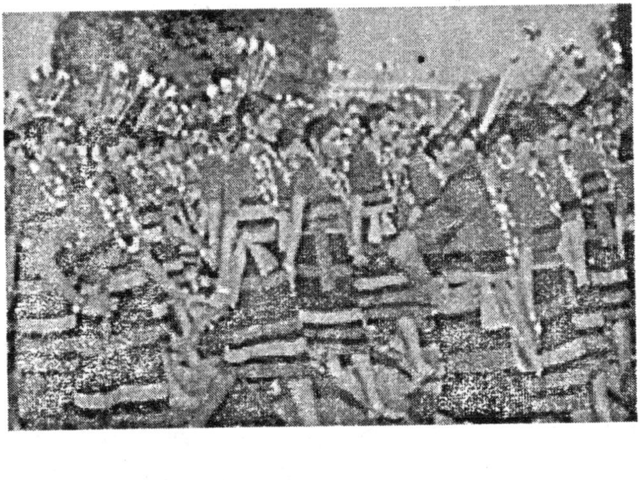

The Lakshwadeep Islands possess its own folk dance form, named the "Lava". The Dadra and Nagar Haveli tribals have their amiable dance form of "Tarpa", in which the dancers tap their feet on moonlit nights, encircling the "Tarpakar" to dance past midnight. This specific Indian tribal dance is heavily accompanied by music. The "Bhavada" dance utilises masks and colourful costumes in the Dadra and Nagar Haveli region. The state of Tripura, with its large tribal population of Riangs, who venerate both tribal and Hindu Gods, survives on agriculture. To certify a good harvest, they mollify Goddess Lakshmi by a dance of young maidens named the "Hawaii".

Andhra Pradesh houses many tribal sects such as the Bhanjaras, Chenchus and Mathuris. In the "Dandaria dance", apart from instruments, time is also maintained by striking sticks one against the other. The Bhanojaras and the Lambadis have costumes of light hues and skirts and blouses studded with small mirrors. Their dance form is called "Bhanjara". This Indian tribal dance kind has agriculture as the elementary theme, with the women going round and round, clapping with gestures suggestive of agrarian occupations.

In Tamil Nadu, the Toda and the Kurumba tribals have rites, rituals and ceremonies, all revolved around agriculture. Kummi and Kolattam are the two most famous folk dances performed by the tribal women of Tamil Nadu. In Kummi, claps maintain the beat, while in Kollattam beat is sustained by striking two sticks. In this form of Indian tribal dance, each dancer possesses two sticks often painted in dazzling colours. In "Pinnal Kolattam", some divisions of the group systematically work up a visual pattern, lacing coloured ropes together, hung from a peg in the ceiling, synchronous with the music.

In course of the dance, the "Pinnal" or the plait is also slowly disentangled to synchronise with the music and the ropes are back to their single-strand shape, precisely when the dance and the music stops. The Muslim community of Tamil Nadu possess a monopoly over the dance called "Pulli Atam", where the men folk dress ornately like a stripped carnivore, with tail, claws, whiskers etc. and dance in the streets. "Karagam" is another Indian tribal dance form of Tamil Nadu dedicated to Goddess Mariamman, the Goddess of health and rain. Men and women balance pots of uncooked rice on their heads to the accompaniment of pipes and drums.

"Kunitha" is a generic term, emblematic of a ritualistic dance in Karnataka. In the "punja Kunitha", a wooden structure is balanced on the head with a deity within it. The "Dollu Kunitha" is a much-admired drum dance of Karnataka. The men play on large drums decorated with colored cloth, slung around their necks, beating on it as they dance. Indian tribal dances are truly varied and umpteen, much like the country`s other aspects, united with diversity.

Dhimsa Dance

Dhimsa Dance is among the Indian tribal dances. It is a dance form of the tribes in the eastern part of Andhra Pradesh, such as Araku Valley near Vizag. The dance is also practised in the tribal regions of Orissa and Madhya Pradesh. The dance is performed during festivals, weddings and also at the time of the "hunting festival" in April when men and women dance for hours. Furthermore, various critics traces the origin of Dhimsa to the Koraput area of Orissa.

The dance is simple and encompasses unique rhythm. Dhimsa Dance presents an enthralling sight as because of the earthy colours of the tribal wear. The costume of the dancer focuses on the movement of the dancers without much emphasis on expression or a literary text. The attire is colourful; shades of red, yellow and green are worn and are called girijans attire themselves. The movements of the dance form are quite expressive. The feet and the hands by the group dominate the dance. An elemental rhythm and animated, quick steps with maneuvers are the distinctive features of the dance form.

Dhimsa Dance provides an impression to the onlookers of a collective performance that matters with each of them complementing the other and merging into a unifying whole. The dance is mainly performed by females and sometime male performers also join in. Duration of each dance remains approximately for 10 minutes. The dance is performed mostly by the farming folk of Andhra Pradesh. The Dhimas Dance of the Porja Caste was considered to be an exclusive Women's Dance. The dance form is dedicated to the welfare of the domestic life. The men and women of the Porja caste perform the Dhimsa Dance with great feeling. It is considered a must for newly-wed because on this day the women pray for a peaceful and happy married life. The dance is performed by women around in unison holding their hands together at wrists.

TRIBAL DANCE FORMS OF KERALA

There are many Tribal Dance forms of Kerala as the state has a cultural heritage of varied tribes.

The state of Kerala possesses a rich cultural heritage because of diversity in the land. It has more than thirty five different types of tribal people and tribal dances like Elelakkaradi, Paniyarkali and Mankali. These dance forms have though witnessed several challenges, yet had survived till the present moments. Besides the classical dances, folk dances, dance dramas and semi-classical dances of the region, Tribal Dance forms of Kerala have also been recognized as a creative expression all over the world. These popular dances of the region reflect the myriad culture, tradition and rituals of the land and reveal all its cultural glory.

Kurumbar Nritham is among the Tribal Dance forms of Kerala. The Waynad district has different types of hill tribes and the kurumbar and the kattunayakar are the most prominent among them. These tribes perform this special type of dance which is related to marriages. The dance is performed both before marriage and after marriage by the members of the families of both the bride and bridegroom. In addition to that the newly wedded couple also performs this dance.

Tribal Dance forms of Kerala include Kaanikkar Nritham. It is a group dance of the kanikkar tribes in Kerala. The steps of the dancers beautifully coordinate with the waving of the hands and beating of drums. Elelakkaradi is a common dance among the Tribals of Kerala called Irulas of Attappadi in Palakkad District. It is a heroic group dance in which almost the whole Irular community of men, women and children participate. The dance resembles the fight of the people against the wild bears which often attack their tribal hamlets. The dance highlights various stages to depict the step by step fight against the wild beasts.

Kaadar Nritham is one of the tribal Dance forms of Kerala where only women participate. This dance form is popular among the Kadar tribes of Cochin Forests and is a primitive form. It is simple but a very elegant dance form. The performers arrange themselves in a semicircle. They hold the tip of their clothes in their hands to the level of the waist while waving it to various rhythms of the dance. Paravalli Kali is also recognised as among the tribal dance forms of Kerela. It is a mixed dance of the aboriginals of dense forest of Travancore area. Both men and women participate in this tribal form of dance. They dance holding arms together, or shoulder to shoulder, linked in a backlock posture. The linked arms swing to the rhythm in a fascinating wavelike movement. The dance develops into variety of pleasing pattern and the men and women change their positions with amazing speed.

Tribal dance forms of Kerela present exclusive forms. Thavala Kali is one such example of the tribal dance where a number of participants, usually boys, jump one above the other in succession while imitating the leaps of the frog.

Kooran Kali and Man Kali are quite similar to one another. Koorankali is a tribal dance where one man takes the role of a wild bear with another enacting the role of hunting dog. The movements are perfectly timed to the rhythmic beats of primitive drums. During the performance, large number of onlookers forms a circle round the two dancers, with cries of joy and occasional clapping of hands and jerky dances. Man kali depicts the episode from Ramayana.

This dance form represents the moment when Sita was being enchanted by Maricha in the guise of a golden deer. The whole drama is enacted in graceful movements.

Paniyar Kali is a masculine dance form performed by the men folks of Panyar tribes of Wayand district. About eight or ten dancers take part in the dance and stand in a circle with hands linked together. They move around with rhythmic flexions of the body. As the dancers gather momentum the circle is swiftly expanded and contracted and the dancers utter peculiar cries which gradually reach to a high pitch. Edaya Nritham is the dance form of men and women from the tribal shepherds. In this dance form one of the shepherds sings. This is repeated in chorus by all the rest. As the singing is continues one of them imitates the special sounds of shepherds driving their sheep. The dance consists of someone of the group crying successively to imitate the wild animals while the other members of the group adeptly bring out the terror on their faces.

Tribal dance forms of Kerela also include Naikar Kali and Gadhika. Naikar Kali is popular ritualistic dance practised among the tribes in Wyanad and Malappuram districts. This is performed as to offer prayers to the family deities during marriage ceremonies. Naikars perform to the tunes of the instruments, the Thappu and the Kuzhal. They dance around in clock-wise and anti-clockwise movements to the accompaniment of the instruments with the jingling anklets around their legs. Gadhika is a ritual dance which is performed by Adiya tribes of Wayanad district. This dance is meant to care ailments and for having a safe delivery of child.

This dance form begins with the principal performer invoking Lord Siva for his help to cure the patients. Several legends are associated with this dance form. According to popular beliefs, once Lord Siva was brought down to earth and he was pleaded by the invocations of the worshippers. The other gods, goddesses were enrolled by the performance. The gods such as Chamundi, Maniamma, Malankali (Siva) and Karinkali were there. The participants include both mostly men. The men dressed as women act to welcome the gods and goddesses arriving in response to the summons from Siva. Mudiyattom also known as Neelilayattom, is another tribal dance in the state.

Tribal Dance forms of Kerela are unique examples of communities that belong to isolated existence, but still preserving their life, customs and manners. Though their dialects and customs are adapted, yet artistic expression evidently reflects the distinct, secluded and primitive social structure and nature of the people. Kerela still witnesses survival in the tribal hamlets of the hilly tracts. Each of these aboriginal tribes presents their own distinct dance tradition and invariably all of them are interwoven with the life of the people.

CHHAU – THE MASKED DANCE FROM PURULIA – WEST BENGAL INDIA

The three styles of Chhau – Seraikella, Purulia and Mayurbhanj – belong to the neighbouring states of Bihar now in Jharkhand, West Bengal and Orissa, in Eastern India. Their location in three different states is the result of the reorganisation of Indian states in 1947. Seraikella and Mayurbhanj were small princely states before Independence and Purulia acquired its name after being discovered in Purulia, West Bengal by the folklorist Late Dr. Ashutosh Bhattacharya in 1960. The same style, however, has an equally strong tradition in the neighbouring villages. The dancers and musicians travel from one place to another to perform this traditional dance.

Chhau dances represent an interesting blend of folk, tribal and classical elements. Like classical dance, there is a certain amount of codification but the dances retain great spontaneity, their movements painting vivid images from everyday life.

Chhau dances are performed by low caste communities and Hinduised tribal groups as part of the rituals associated with the great Spring Festival, Chaitra Parva, celebrated over the adjoining districts of the states bordering West Bengal, Bihar (now in Jharkhand) and Orissa in Eastern India during mid - April-May. All styles of Chhau dances are represented at the Spring Festival, Chaitra Parva, which is an ancient tradition that plays a vital social and religious role in the life of the region.

Of the three styles of Chhau, Purulia is the most robust and virile. Unlike Seraikella, Purulia Chhau never depended on royal patronage so it retains its vigorous folk character. With great gusto the dancers plant their feet forcefully on the ground and freeze in postures of encounter and challenge, bent knee foot stamping, short vertical jumps and full circle spins characterise this style as does the violent juggling of shoulders and shivering of the upper torso.

Purulia dancers wear elaborate costumes – the embroidered velvet jacket and striped baggy trousers are a mixture of the Jatra folk theatre and 19th century theatrical costumes.

The performances take place in the open ground platform. It begins in the late evening and may continue whole night. The audiences sit on the ground encircling the performers in separate groups of men and women.

The music that accompanies Purulia Chhau is played on three instruments: A Shenai – wind instrument, the Dhamsa kettle drum and the Dholak or Dhol, a drum carried on a shoulder strap that is beaten by a thin stick at one end and by the hand at the other end. The dholak player acts as a kind of picador or ring master to the dancers, running forward and shouting as if to goads them into dancing.

At the beginning of the performance the musicians play a lively welcome tune of Shenai and the drums beat rhythmically. Lord Ganesh (The Hindu God with elephant's head and four arms) is evoked before. He actually appears in the opening dance recitals. He is followed by epic heroes, other Gods and Goddesses with multi-coloured masks gleaming with tinsel, equipped with extra arms or heads (as required) made of wood or indigenous materials.

The mask is an integral part of Purulia Chhau Dance. It liberates the dancer from the limiting influence of the face and puts a greater burden on the movements of the body. The body moves it bring the mask alive. Purulia masks are rustic; their wide-open eyes give a sense of speed and gusto. In both cases a headdress complements the mask.

The masks are made of pulp and indigenous colours and decorated with peacock feathers, jaris and hairs. The masks are fascinating products of superb craftsmanship.

Most Chhau themes are drawn from the two great Indian epics – the Ramayana and the Mahabharata as well as the mythology of the Puranas.

The Chhau Dance Group consists of 12 + 1 persons of 8 Dancers, 4 Drummers & Instrumentalists and 1 Programme Manager cum Tour Co-ordinator.

KARMA TRIBAL DANCE IN INDIA

India is an umbrella for the vibrant tribal set, which describes the colorful art of living a life. The Swaying body and clapping hands follows the rhythm of drum-beats and speaks about the many dances involved in the tribal culture. One popular tribal dance form is the Karma type, highly performed by Adivasis residing at the interior of

Chhattisgarh and Madhya Pradesh in India. Tribal groups like Gonds, the Baigas and the Oraons in Chattisgarh are masters in this jazzing art. Other tribes of Madhya Pradesh like the Thumki, the Payri, the Chhalla and Jhumki are also seen to have gain momentum in this folk dance.

The traditional dance is preformed specially during the Karma Festival held as per the Hindu month of Bhadrapada(August). Folks believe that this dance is a way to pay tribute to Lord Karma. Both men and women arrange themselves in two rows and follow the rhythmic steps, directed by the singer group. The Karma tribal dance marks the end of the rainy season and the advent of spring season. Participants cuts the branches of Karam tree and thereafter dancing session follows the insertion of this branches in the dancing ground called " akhara". The branches are named as Karam Raja and tribal believes that this activity offers them with good fortune through out the year.

The Karma Dance gets its tempo with the quick beating of drums and loud style of singing. The dance manifest the arrival of flower, fruit and freshness thereby marking India evermore beautiful.

Banjara: the tribal gypsies of India, a source of nomadic tribal bellydance.

Cholis are significantly more used in Tribal belly dance as coined bras. Cholis organically come from India and became very popular among the American Tribal Style and middle eastern tribal style costuming.

The ancient art of middle eastern dance has a long and colorful history. It began with the many fertility cults of the ancient world, and in the temples of ancient India. The existence of various nomadic groups of professional entertainers, and groups specifically identified with Gypsies (Rom), provided for the cross-culturation and transmission of these dances.

The history of middle eastern dance is intertwined with that of Gypsies, in their various guises in each country they travelled through. They came from India and spread through Persia, Turkey, Arabia, Egypt, Greece, and through much of Europe. To this day, many nomadic women in the Near East bear hand and ankle tattoos thought to be Gypsy in design, often a universal symbol meaning a traveler. This intense tribal pride is significant in maintaining their cultural identity throughout their travels, and is characteristic of true Gypsies.

India is a vast country with many different tribes, dances and music.

Specially the dances of the Punjab, the Sind region, Rajastan and Madhya Pradesh are close to the origins of bellydance. Done by wandering gypsy tribes, the dances and costumes tell of their islamic influence or in other words: the Mughal culture.

The sophisticated art of the Hindustani gypsy dancing girls did inspire the modern-day Bollywood music and dance. Here bollywood star Aruna Irani in typical gypsy dress as Nisha, a gypsy dancer, in a movie of the sixties about a band of gypsies moving and living in a *Caravan*.

The Banjara tribe is the most colorful of any tribal group in India, the original habitants of Rajastan. Banjaras have an unique costume and embroidery style. As nomads of the Thar desert, they live in Central and of Western India. One of the dances of these tribe in Rajasthan is dancing with a jar on the head. The colorful dances of Garbha or Garbi and the Dandia are danced on the occasion of the festival of Dussehra in honour of Durga. The Mother-Godess Durga stands for the good in the world and the femininity or shakti. The dresses are ornamented with mirrors called *shishador*. Red is the dominant color. The costumes on the picture are pretty old as the use of large and irregular mirrors reflects.

The clothes and the jewelery of this particular tribe is now very popular amongst tribal bellydance style troupes. Their beautiful silver jewellery and embroidered costumes and colorful choly are a feast for the eyes. Every part of the body is ornamented with jewellery, with it's own symbolic significane. Silver is considered more precious than gold. Banjara dances differ from occasion to occasion. On the Rakhi festival, the Banjara's perform the Lehangi.

Mohiniyattam dance or dance of the enchantress, is a traditional dance from Kerala, South Indian. With hip movements and ritual expressions by the hand palm and fingers (also called mudras) it is an ancient dance done by tge Devadasis in temples

DANCE FORMS

The primitive inhabitants of Kerala, the tribal people are scattered in the jungles and hills of Malabar, Kochi and Travancore. There are about 35 different types of the tribals, chief among them being the Kurichiyar, Nayadi, Mullakurumbar, Uralikurumbar, Paniya, Mudaga, Irula, Ernadar, Kadar, Muthuvan, Kanikkar, Uralees, Paliyan, Malavedan, Vettuvar, Eravallam, Veda and Malayan. They are unique examples of communities in isolated existence, still preserving their life, customs and manners almost untarnished by the advancing waves of urban civilization. Though adapted to different dialects and customs, their artistic expression evidently reflects the distinct, secluded and primitive social structure and nature of the people and it still survives as virile a state as ever in the tribal hamlets of the hilly tracts.

Each of these aboriginal tribes has its own distinct dance traditions and invariably all of them are interwoven with the life of the people who dance it, so much so that it seems that some of their daily tasks are given to rhythmic pattern. In the background of mystry shrouded nature, tribal celebrations originate and the dances which work up intoxicating excitement physical expressions of their joys and griefs, hopes and fears.

In some cases the dancing is extremely simple and

consists of little more than meaningless shuffling of the feet or waving of the hands. At other times it is mere swaying of the body to the clapping of hands or beating of primitive drums to mark time. Yet another form shows only the monotonous movement of the hands and feet. But, generally speaking, a wide range of movement involving all parts of the body, the head, back hips, arms, fingers and the feet and even facial muscles are utilized in tribal dances.

There are very complicated tribal dances as well in which dancing harmonises gesture, expressing the whole gamut of sentiment, where rhythm is kept by swaying the body and intricate steps executed with adept foot-work. Usually the dances have a slow beginning, but gather momentum and work up to a heavy tempo of the vociferous climax of the drums, and the ecstacy of the ever-mounting rhythm of spontaneous music. Many of these dances are heroic or martial in character.

Some tribes have songs to accompany their dances. Either the dancers themselves sing or the onlookers sing and thus participate. Special musical instruments are sometimes used, but the drum is almost an indispensable feature. The costumes of the dancers vary from approximate nudity to full attire and ornaments which are extremely colourful and gaudy.

Like all tribal arts, Kerala's tribal dances are spontaneous. It is the most direct expression of the inner most spirit of a people and the instinct of rhythm is as natural and basic as human nature.

Some of the more well known tribal dances of Kerala are *Elelakkaradi, Kadarkali, Kurumbarkali, Paniyarkali, Edayarkali, Mudiyattam* and *Vedarkali.*

Tribal people constitute an important segment of the teeming millions in our country. India has the second largest tribal sects in Kerala, the *Paniya, Adiya, Urali, Kattunaikka, Irula, Muduva, Aranadan* are the prominent tribal communities.

The tribals artistic expressions, after all, are pure, innocent human sentiments pertaining to primordial agrarian life.

ELELAKKARADI

This is a highly heroic group-dance in which almost the whole community of men, women and children participate. The dance is very common with the tribals called *Irular* of Attappadi in Palakkad district. The dance brings out the fight of the people against the wild bears which very often attack their tribal hamlets. Here the dancers move out in rhythmic steps, with vociferous shouts and war cries and keep time to the beatings of the primitive drums. The various stages in the fight against the wild beasts are very well presented.

KAADAR NRITHAM

Only women partake in this primitive dance of the Kaadar tribes of the forests of Kochi area. The performers arrange themselves in a semicircle. They hold the tip of their clothes in their hands to the level of the waist and wave it to various rhythms of the dance. It is a very simple but elegant tribal dance in slow steps.

KURUMBAR NRITHAM

Waynad district had different types of hill tribes of which the *Kurumbar* and the *Kattunayakar* are the most prominent. They perform a special type of dance which is staged in connection with marriages. Before marriage, the members of the families of both the bride and bridegroom and after marriage the newly-wedded couple perform this dance. After the return of the bridegroom with his bride to his family, all the members of his household and the newly wedded again repeat the dance.

KAANIKKAR NRITHAM

This is a group dance of the Kanikkar tribes. The dance

is performed as a ritual offering. The steps of the dancers perfectly synchronise with the waving of the hands and the beating of the drums.

PANIYAR KALI

Paniyar are another set of tribals inhabiting the hilly forests of Waynad district. Their dance is highly masculine and only men participate. Here the dancers numbering about eight or ten stand in a circle with hands linked together. They move around with rhythmic flexions of the body and while moving stamp the ground in perfect rhythm to the loud beat of the primitive percussion instruments called *Karu, para, udukku, etc.* As the dance gathers momentum the circle is swiftly expanded and contracted and the dancers utter peculiar cries which gradually run up to a high pitch.

MAN KALI

This tribal dance is of two kinds. In one version, the Ramayana episode in which Sita is being enchanted by Maricha in the guise of a golden deer is enacted in graceful movements.

In the second type, one man takes the role of a deer while another that of a hunter. The deer hopes about and jumps around. The hunter follows in close steps and his movements and gestures suggest drawing the bow, aiming it, hurling the spear, brandishing some wooden log, etc. The whole dance is performed to the rhythm of wild percussion instruments.

PARVALLIKALI

It is mixed dance of the aboriginals of the dense forest of *Travancore* area in which both men and women participate. They dance holding arms together, or shoulder to shoulder, linked in a back lock posture. The dance develops into variety of pleasing pattern, in which the men and women change their positions with amazing speed. The entire group of dancers sing songs and move in swift rhythm in a circle. The linked arms swing to the rhythm in a fascinating wavelike movement.

MUDIYATTOM

Mudiyattom, also known as *Neelilyattom*, is a tribal dance in which only women partake. The woman stand on small wooden blocks and the dance begins with slow and simple movements of the body which culminate in graceful movements of the head. The uncombed hair of the participants flow down and swing in rhythmic waves. The instruments used are *karu, maram, para, kokkaro* etc.

KOORANKALI

Kooranlkali is another tribal dance which is similar to Mankali. Here one man takes the role of a wild bear with another enacting the role of a hunting dog. The movements are perfectly timed to the rhythmic beats of primitive drums. While this is going on, the large number of onlookers who form a circle round the two dancers, shout wild cries of joy with occasional clapping of hands and jerky dances.

THAVALAKALI

Thavalakali is a tribal dance in which a number of participants, usually boys, jump one above the other in succession, imitating the leaps of the frog.

EDAYA NRITHAM

Edaya nritham is the dance of the tribal shepherds. Both men and women participate. One of the shepherds sing. This is repeated in chorus by all the rest. As the singing is going on, one of them imitates the special sounds of shepherds driving their sheep.

The dance as such consists of someone of the group trying successively to imitate the wild animals that try to attack the sheep and also the thief who tries to robe them while the other members of the group very adeptly bring out the terror on the faces of the lambs and their mournful wailings.

NAIKKAR KALI

This is popular among the tribes in Wyanad and Malappuram districts. It is more ritualistic than entertainment oriented. This is performed as pooja to family deities and during marriages.

When the instruments, *Thappu* and *Kuzhal* start playing, the *naikars* begin their performance. With jingling anklets round their legs, they dance round in clock-wise and anti-clockwise movements to the accompaniment of the instruments. In between they shout 'Hoy Hoy'.

GADHIKA

Gadhika is a ritual dance performed by *Adiya* tribes of Wayanad district. The art form is meant to cure ailments. The performance is also done as part of a ritual for having a safe delivery of child.

NATU GADHIKA

Pleaded by invocations of the worshippers. The other gods, goddesses were enrolled by the performance. These gods include *Chamundi, Maniamma, Malankali (Siva) and Karimkali.* Simultaneously other actors dressed in colourful costumes also move centralistic which is titled with a small structure that resembles a temple. The participants include men dressed as women whose function is to welcome the gods and goddesses arriving in response to the summons from Siva.

2

Tribal Dances of Andhra Pradesh

In Andhra there are nearly thirty-three kinds of foresters, hill men and tribals. All have, their own dances. These dances can be broadly classified into three heads (i) Religious dances (ii) Social dances (iii) Dance as a past time.

Kuchipudi, one of the classical dance forms of the South had its origin in Andhra Pradesh.

Peacock Dance of the Khonds

The Khonds, also called Samanlas are the most backward hill men dwelling in the inaccessible hilly region of Visakhapatnam and Srikakulam districts. During weddings and festival which falls in the month of April, the Khonds perform the peacock dance. Pirodi, a kind of flute and the tinkling bells around the ankles are the only musical accompaniments. All the dancers put on white dhotis, tie anklets called Muyyangam, wear turbans, made of locally growing grass and tugged with colourful rags and fasten bunches of peacock feathers behind at their waists which look like peacock tails whenever they bend forward.

All the dancers stand in two rows in the beginning and imitate the cry of peacock. They form a circle and bend forward from their knees so as to look like a dancing peacock. After paying obeisance to mother earth and the Sun god they commence dancing. Putting their palms to their right legs move their left legs rhythmically, the anklets produce jingling sounds. They step forward and backward while the pirodi produces sonorous motes sitting, circling, stepping, bending and waving kerchiefs in their right hands, they look like dozens of peacocks dancing joyously in a circle. This includes gestures of the bridegroom going to the bride's house.

THE MANGO DANCE OF THE KONDA REDDIS

The Hill Reddis or Konda Reddis also called the Reddis of the Bison hills dwell in Khamman, East Godavari and West Godavari districts. These parts are famous for mangoes. Before plucking the mangoes, the Konda Reddis have a ceremonial festival with a community Dance. They neither decorate nor paint their body like the Gusadis. As an act of worship to Mutyalamma and Konda devata, they dance rhythmically to the accompaniment of drums. This dance commences during the night, with a gentle beat of drums.

Three to four women hand in hand with the castanet like sound of dry nuts join the dance. The men and women both join the dance but they form separate groups. Leaning towards the left they circumambulate around the place. The women, while tapping the ground with the foot, take four steps forward. This is done in a particular manner. Stepping forward with the right foot four times, leaning towards one side, they come back with one step in the same manner. The circle of men and women moving rhythmically to the centre and retreating with waving arms and the clatter of nuts provide a fascinating pattern for the dance.

Keeping the feet apart and jumping with the right and left foot alternately with the other foot forward is another feature of this dance. The dance steps of the men are different from those of the women. The men while stepping forward, put the right foot first and bring the left foot up to the heel of right foot. This facilitates stepping forward again with the right foot. The drummers and other instrumentalists stand in the centre in the beginning, later they join in the dances and step accordingly forward and backward along with the whole group. The two types of drums used as accompaniment provide regular rhythm to this foot work. When drum beats quicker, the dance also gets momentum and vigour.

After feasting about midnight; men, women and children again begin to dance. They also sing songs invoking Mutyalamma and the hill gods and goddesses. This singing has some religious significance. The song comes to an end by the time the ritual dance reaches its climax. The groups break up and dancing, circling and jumping in frenzy, again form into groups. This dance continues till the next morning and concludes when fatigue overtakes them.

Dimsa Dance of Araku Valley

The Araku valley is the most charming hilly region in Visakhapatnam district. Valmiki, Bagata, Khond and Rotia tribes inhabit this valley and other areas of this district. The favourite dance of these tribes is Dimsa which is performed by old and young men and women, during the month of chaitra i.e. in March/April, during weddings and other festivals. During festivals people go from one village to another to participate in the dance and are honoured with community feasts. People of different villages enjoy such festivities and dances called 'Sankidi Kelbar'. Dimsa

Dance not only provides amusement to the dancers and spectators but also develops friendship and fraternity between people of different villages. The instruments accompanying Dimsa are mori Kiridi, tudumu, duppu and jodukommulu. There are eight varieties of the Dimsa Dance.

(i) Boda Dimsa- It is a worship dance in honour of the village goddess. Men on the right side and women on the left side form two rows and hold one another firmly with their hands over their backs. The first man in the right row, with a bunch of peacock feathers in his hands in rhythmical steps takes the lead as a hero and the last person in the left row joins him. Then all the dancers, once again to the sounds of the anklets move zigzag as in a serpent dance in a circle, crying Hari and Hui. In mirth they go round and come back in to the rows.

(ii) Gunderi Dimsa or 'Usku Dimsa'- A male member of the dancing troupe sings out an invitation to the females to dance with him. The males and females with firm steps moving forward and backwards, stride in a circle. This is a vigorous and exciting dance.

(iii) Goddi Beta Dimsa - Bowing down and lifting up their heads, the tribal troupes dance as if they are picking up stones. Bending forward and rising up with a swing, they go forward twenty-five steps and come back in the same manner. This is repeated four to five times.

(iv) Potar - Tola Dimsa - This dance symbolises picking up leaves. Half of the dancers stand side by side in a row. The rest stand behind the first row in the same manner and keep their hands on the shoulders of the people standing before them. Turning their heads to the right and left, the two rows march forward and backward.

(v) Bhag Dimsa- This dance is meant as an instruction on how to escape from a tiger's attack. Half of the troupe form a circle hand in hand. They stand on their toes, bowing and raising their heads. Moving round swiftly, the rest enter the circle and form a 'serpent coil'. This is repeated several times.

(vi) Natikari Dimsa- This is a solo dance performed by valmikis on Deepavali in particular and other tribals during other festivals in general.

(vii) Kunda Dimsa- In this the dancers push each other with their shoulders while singing rhythmically.

(viii) Baya Dimsa. This is a dance of the tribal magician (gamachari) when he is possessed by the village goddess. All the villagers surround the magician with their heads bowed and imitate him. This continues till the magician returns to normalcy from his trance.

The united community view point is the essential feature of these tribal dances. Without any discrimination of caste and creed, age and sex, the whole community participate in these dances.

The community development programmes have affected their way of life and the dance forms, which essentially belongs to their cultural heritage. All the dances conform to the rhythm of either Aditala or Rupakatala.

The Gusadi Dance of Gonds

Deepavali is the biggest festival for the Raj Gonds of Adilabad district. As the harvest is over and the season is cool and congenial the Gonds dressed in colourful costumes and decòrated with ornaments go to neighbouring villages in troupes, singing and dancing. Such troupes are called Dandari dance troupes. Each troupe consist of twenty to forty members. 'Gusadi' is a part of Dandari and consists of two to five members. This starts on the full moon day and goes on till the fourteenth day of the dark fortnight of Deepavali.

Each member puts on a turban of peacock feathers and horns of the deer, artificial beard and moustaches and goatskin to cover the body. Dappu, tudumu, pipri and kalikom are the accompaniments. The Dandari troupe dance accompanied by beats of gumela reaches its climax with regulated steps and rhythm in a circular form.

The Dandari dance starts with stepping slowly towards the left side and swinging the right foot on to the left foot at every step. Every dancer has two small sticks in his hands.

First everyone strikes the two sticks in his own hands, then strike at the sticks of the person on the right side then strike his own sticks and then the sticks of the person on the left side. In this way, with steps and striking together of sticks held in hands they play kolattam and come back to the original position.

Then they bend down and touch the ground with their sticks and step on to the four sides. This is paying obeisance to the gods. After this they put into order their circular form and lay down the sticks. Then they sing and clap their hands. They sing a group song in duet, one group singing the first line and the second group singing the second line of the song.

While this is going on, the Gusadi troupe intrudes into the circle with peacock feathered turbans, artificial beards and moustaches, goat skins as covers, strings of cowries and beads around the neck, tinkling bells on wrists, white stripes and dots on the bodies, with modesty pieces around the waists and poles in their hands they enter the circle.

After the scattering of the Dandaris, the former raising their hands, and swaying and jerking to the accompanying sounds of the bells and cowries on their bodies.

It present a dreadful scene to the on lookers. They jump hither and thither and they utter war cries and with vehement motion and frenzied laughter they frighten the boys and come up on the spectators. They also touch the waists of the spectators with the poles in their hands and tickle them.

After some time they dance rhythmically, stepping forward and backward and hither and thither and also zigzag to the accompaniment of instruments. Lastly, the hosting villagers invite them and wash their feet.

LAMBADI DANCE

Lambadi is the semi - nomadic tribe that is spread all over Andhra. They are also known as Banjaras or Sugalis. Their dances are inspired by the movements associated with daily tasks like harvesting, planting and sowing. The costumes, embroidered with glass-beads and shining discs are picturesque; matched by the abundance of ornate jewellery worn by them.

The jingling brass anklets, the hanging cowry bunches and the ivory bangles from wrists to elbows provide a natural rhythm to their dances.

Dussehra, Deepavali and Holi are the festive occasions when the Banjaras go from house to house dancing and receiving alms. Twenty to thirty Banjara women dressed in colourful costumes with shining brass vessels filled with water either on heads or waists present a group dance. The graceful movements of their waving hands and supple waists provide a feast to the onlookers.

Siddi Dance

The Siddis present tribal dances during marriages and other festive occasions. Their dances depict the tribal warfare of their home land in all its ferocity. Armed with shining sword and matchlock and dressed in their exotic primitive costumes, they dance with vigour and force.

In rural Andhra some folk dance forms are confined to certain regions, some dance forms are common to all the regions.

Tappeta Gundlu

Tappeta gundlu is a folk dance confined to the coastal districts of Srikakulam, Vijayanagaram and Vishakhapatnam. This was originally performed by cowherds and shepherds as a ritualistic dance propitiating the rain god and their favourite deity Gangamma. While dancing they sing devotional songs on Sri Krishna, Dasavataras and on goddess Gangamma besides other folk songs and narratives.

Tappeta or gundlu is a small percussion instrument in the shape of a drum hanging on the chest and tied to the sides and neck of the players. A troupe consisting of eight to sixteen artistes sing and dance in circles beating with their hands the drums tied to their chests. The players tie jingling bells to their ankles. They put on tight knickers stitched with jingling bells all over. They tie colourful clothes around their waists and long loin clothes hanging up to their feet in front as well as at the back resembling two tails.

This dance requires skill and muscle power. The artistes exhibit rare skills in acrobatics while dancing. The drum beats, the sounds of jingling bells tied to their ankles and the sounds of the bells stitched to their shorts blend harmoniously with the different gaits and steps of the artistes. Their repertoire constitutes twenty to thirty gatibhedas. The dance, styles along with a variety of songs composed in consonance with the dance styles.

All dancers sing pallavi of a song or a narrative following their troupe leader. While dancing, the artistes, eight in a group, stand one above the other on the thighs and shoulders in the shape of a gopuram or a tree with its branches hanging. They lie down and move like the hands of a clock.

They stand one above the other on an earthen pot with tumblers full of water on their heads. They whirl fast and fall down with a heavy thud. They come out of their dancing circle and exhibit shoulder and limb movements as in the Bhangra dance of Punjab. The beating of drums, dancing and singing always goes on.

Urumulu (Thunder Dance)

Urumulu or thunder dance is found only in Anantapuram district. The instrument employed in this dance is called urumu. It is a percussion instrument which sounds like thunder. The instrument is made out of brass or bell metal - a hollow round pipe. Both sides are covered with goat skin fixed on to iron rings and tightened with ropes at the top of the drum. It hangs from the left shoulder on the belly of the artiste and it is tied to the right side of the waist. The left side of the instrument is rubbed with a thin stick and the right side is beaten with a thick stick.

The urumu dancers belong to the scheduled caste. They are a pious and virtuous group of people who observe religious austerity and worship goddess Akkamma. They abstain from drinking and eating meat. They present urumu dance to please their deity. It is a ceremonial dance. They, move in circles adopting different styles and foot steps and play on urumu. They put on big turbans and strings of beads or coins like metal pieces around their necks.

They smear their faces with turmeric and also put on Namam on their foreheads. They wear long shirts covering from neck to feet and an upper garment hanging from both shoulders. While dancing they sing devotional songs on Lord Kadiri Narasimhaswami, Dasavataras and goddess Akkamma.

Butta Bommalata

Marionette play is the oldest surviving art form in India. The marionette's or puppets are made of different materials. Butta Bommalu are made of bamboo, tamarind seed paste, paper, cattle dung or husk and hay. The figures are coloured according to the tradition and used for plays.

It is made up to waist only and hollow inside. The dolls are three to four times bigger than the human figures. A coloured cloth is tied around the doll at the waist that covers the player who enter into it. There is a hole in the doll at the navel through which the artiste can see the outside world. Figures of Siva and Parvati,Vishnu and Lakshmi, Garuda and Hanuman, Radha and Krishna are very common in Butta Bommalata.

It is presented at festive gatherings, car festivals, marriage ceremonies, Navaratri celebrations, Ganesh immersion festivals and recently in election campaigns. These puppets are large enough to serve as full masks for men and women who dance to the rhythm of a Dappu or Mridangam. Band, Dhole, Sonnayi are used as accompaniments in the Butta Bommalata. The troupe consist of at least ten members four of whom are in the puppets and dance, four who play instruments, one instructor and the troupe leader. This is only a dumb dance, accompanied only by the sounds of instruments.

Goravayyalu

Gorava or blankets. The priests among Kurubas are known as Goravas. They dedicate one male member to the god Srisaila Mallikarjuna when he grows up he is initiated into the Moilara cult by a Ganachari and trained in the lore Kuruba or Kuruma is a sub caste of shepherds who tend sheep and weave wool ritualistic music and dance by a senior Gorava. During the festivals and Kalyanotsavas of their family deities Goravayyalu present their ritualistic dance with great fanfare. During the other days they move from one place to another singing the ballads of Mallanna and other Saiva panegyrics, beg alms and bless the devotees.

They put on a long black coat made out of sheep wool with white strips, a big triangular jar cap made out of bear's skin. One upper cloth hanging from both shoulders, another cloth serving as a waist band. A bag made of deer skin containing the sacred turmeric called Bandaru to be offered to the devotees, a brass cup tied to the waist for drinking milk or pancamritam. They wear strings of cowries around their necks, tie jingling bells to their ankles. They hold a damaru in the right hand and a flute in the left hand.

They play these instruments when they dance. While dancing they move in circles and jump forward and backward like fighting rams. They bark at each other like fighting dogs. They call themselves faithful dogs of god. Mallari or Mailaru. They drink milk or Pancamritam contained in the brass cups placed on the ground like dogs kneeling on the ground without holding the cups with their hands. The remnants are shared by devotees as prasadam when they perform this ritual dance in the temple precincts they pierce their cheeks, calf wrist with iron pikes and blued as offering to the deity and beat themselves with big hunters called veratallu. This dance is purely ritualistic performed during religious occasions.

Garaka Dance (Vessel Dance)

Garaga means a pot or vessel. The dance performed with a vessel on the head is known as Garaganrityam. This is very popular in Karnataka and Tamil Nadu. This dance was performed as a ritual by Asadis during propitiating ceremonies of village goddesses. In Andhra this is popular in the coastal districts and the border districts of Karnataka and Tamil Nadu.

In olden days the priest in trance known as Ganachary used to dance without any make up for himself, with a decorated earthen pot on his head in-front of the temple of a village goddess or along with her retinue in procession to the beats of Dappu. It is a strong percussion instruments. In course of time the Garaga dance has acquired many attractive adjuncts in make up and dance styles. Brass vessels covered with colourful cloths, decorated with vermilion and turmeric are held on the heads by the artistes when they dance. The mouth of the brass vessel is covered with a five hooded serpent made in brass or bronze.

The dancers put on colourful clothes and hold a bunch of margosa leaves symbolic of Shakti worship. The adept Dappu players produce varying beats in Trisara, caturasra and other gatis and the garaga dancers dance and produce the same sounds with the jingling bells tied to their ankles. The artistes maintain the balance of the vessels on their heads by without moving their heads though their bodies and limbs move very fast. They have introduced many nuances and acrobatics in their dance styles for attracting the spectators. They lie down on their bellies and pick up coins and sticks with their lips. They stand facing each other on one leg and make a knot with each others leg and dance to the drum beats. They also play kolatam striking at each others stick. All these while maintaining the balance of the vessels on their heads.

Vira Natyam (Heroic Dance)

Viranatyam also known as Virabhadra natyam is a community or the traditional ceremonial dance that used to be presented in the Siva and Virabhadra temples when Virasaivism was at its Zenith. Veerabhadra, the destroyer of Daksha's sacrifice is said to be the originator of this dance. Holding a sword in one hand and a shield in another hand the devotee dances and plays steps according to the beat of Viramam. It is a big percussion instrument which produces sharp and piercing sounds. Viramam sounds resembles the sounds of war drums and trumpets and Viranatyam resembles Tandavanrityam in its force and vigour. Dhole, Tashamarpa and Sonmayi are also played during the Viranatyam. At the time of Lingodbhava on the sacred day of Sivaratri, these artistes present Urdhava Tandavam, a special type of dance.

Viranatyam is performed by Viramushti, Jangam, Balija and Devanga communities of Virasaiva cult. In Telangana, Viranatyam is presented by Viramushti and Jangam communities during the festivals in Virabhadreswara temple at Kovari and Kottakonda while offering Virabhadra palleram to the deity. A big plate with burning oil or camphor flames is held in both the hands from palms up to elbows and shown before the deity as an offering.

The dancers also recite poems called Khadgalu in praise of Virabhadra and his exploits. The artistes wield swords while singing these panegyrics. It is a vigorous and awful dance with long steps and upward movements of legs and hands. In devotional frenzy and fervor, the artistes also pierce their tongues, cheeks, eyelids, throats and lips with spears and spikes of different denominations called Ekanarasam, Kantimarasam, Kanthanarasam and Sulanarasam. They bleed and dance in frenzy. This ceremonial dance has now gained wide popularity as a folk art due to the many nuances introduced in the dance styles.

Kolatam

Kolatam is a play with sticks. This is known as Hallisaka and Dandarasaka in Sanskrit. In olden days females used to play Kolatam in temple halls as a devotional offering. Now the Kolatam played by males is a folk art form.

A troupe consists of twenty to forty members or the least eight members. There are even numbers of players and a leader in every troupe. The troupe leader is called Pennuddi or Kolanna Pantulu or Garuva. He controls and leads the troupe. A pair of two players is called Uddi in which one is called Rama and the other is Lakshmana. All the players form a big circle in the beginning and change into two circles one in another. The leader along with the Mridangam, flute, harmonium and cymbal players, stand in the middle of the inner circle.

Each player holds two sticks one in each hand with coloured strings or bells tied to their ends. As soon as the leader signals, pairs in the circle starts moving with a prayer to Lord Ganesha. The leader then cries out the rhythm Etlugada and begins a song. The songs are in different rhymes and beats. They may be prayers, duets, descriptions or narratives delineating Bhakti, Sringara, Karuna and Virarasa. The variety in steps is called Kopulu.

There are 50 kinds of kopulu as maximum and minimum number ranges from six to twelve. When the troupe leader sings the first line of the song the players sing the second line and strike the sticks moving or jumping forward and backward in the circles. The leader whistles and changes the speed to a high crescendo. This is called 'Usi'. The players accordingly move with fast steps maintaining the speed for some time and stop with Muktayimpu. The troupe leader then takes up another kopu and the kolatam continues with different style.

There is a special type of Kolatam called 'Jada Kolatam'or veni Kolatam'. This is more popular in Karnataka. The troupe consisting of 12 to 18 players holding coloured strings or ropes tied above to a pole or branch of a tree form into a circle. The circle's movements inside and outside are so well timed and executed that the ropes hanging from the top become plaited to form a Jada or veni. when the troupe dances anticlockwise the ropes are unwound again, colourful ribbons on platforms during ceremonial occasions.

Chiratala Bhajana

Chiratala Bhajana or Chekka Bhajana resembles Kolattam very closely in its movements, steps, dance and style and songs except that the players hold Chiratalu instead of sticks. All the technical terms like jattu, Garidi, Uddi, Kopu, Ettugada, Muktayimpu, Usi are common to both Kolattam and Chiratala Bhajana. Chiratalu, a pair of wooden pieces chiseled and riveted with jingling bells and metal pieces, produces metallic and rattling sound. The two pieces can be held in a palm like a single piece by inserting the thumb and middle finger into the rings fixed in the centre on the top side of the wooden pieces. By opening and closing the palm the two pieces strike each other and produces musical sound.

In Kolattam each player hold two sticks one in each hand, in Chiratala Bhajana the players hold a pair of Chiratalu in one hand and a colourful handkerchief in another which he waves while jumping and dancing. The kolattam kopus are of short duration where as the Chiratala Bhajana kopus are of long duration facilitating narration of episodes from Epics and Puranas. There are nearly 100 kinds of kopus depicting variety in the steps. In modern times long narratives have been divided into small bits with different gatis and styles. In olden days lamp posts used to be erected in the middle of the circle of players. Now troupe leader stands in the middle and sings the narrative playing cymbals or Chiratalu.

A troupe consisting of 10 to 20 members forms into a circle while the leader who stands in the centre begins the bhajan, directing the troupe. All members follow him. The commencing steps are known as Adi Adugu (beginning steps). This is compulsory item. The other steps are known as Potu Adugu, Kuppadugu, Kulukula Adugu, Joku Adugu, Nemili Adugu, Gurappu Adugu, Uyyala Adugu. The players hang garlands in their necks and tie jingling bells to their ankles, they also tie colourful waist bands.

Dappu Dance

Dappu is a percussion instrument. It is a counterpart of Dandora of North India. It is also called Tappeta in coastal Andhra. It is made out of calf hide fixed to the margosa wooden structure in a circular shape. It is beaten with two sticks one thin and the other thicker.

The form belongs exclusively to Harijans. Dappu dance is a vigorous type of dance as the Dappu is a powerful percussion instrument. A troupe consisting of ten to twenty artistes presents Dappu dance during marriage processions, car festivals of deities and village fairs and festivals. Tiger steps, bird steps, horse steps are some of the styles of dance movements presented in the Dappu dance. Sometimes the songs sung verge on obscenity as in Lella Patalu to settle old scores.

The beat of the Dappu and the foot work of the dancers synchronise with each other so perfectly that from a slow moving, low-beating rhythm, it reaches its climax with the frantic drums keeping pace with the dazzling foot work by the dancers. They play several kinds of rhythms like Trisra, Chaturasa, Mirsa, Khandagati, Sankeerna, jatis, comprising seven type of beats. They follow different kinds of dance, leaping from one side to another with complicated foot work. They tie jingling bells to their ankles.

Spectators throw coins on a Dappu placed on the ground. when the players around that Dappu beat their drums vigorously, the Dappu placed on the ground responds to the sound vibrations and the coins over it dance and slide down to be picked up as a reward by the artistes.

PULI VESHAM OR TIGER DANCE

This is a popular one-man dance performed during Dussehra and Muharram festivals. An able bodied man with a narrow strip of cloth around the waist, and the whole body painted with stripes like a tiger and elaborate make-up, sporting a long tail, dances vigorously in tiger like strides and wild jumps. A Dappu or Mridangam provides the rhythm. In some parts of Andhra a second man behind the dancer carries the artificial but heavy tail tied to the back of the dancer. The dancer lifts a brass pot full of water with his teeth depicting an unruly tiger's devouring nature and strength.

Gobbi Dance

This is a popular dance in coastal Andhra during the Samkranti festival. The courtyards of all houses are cleaned and decorated with different kinds of rangavallis.

Gobbillu i.e. balls of cow dung are placed in the middle of these designs and worshipped with flowers, kumkum and turmeric.

During evenings young girl's gather around these gobbillu to dance and sing. This dance is a derived form of Garba described in dance treatises.

Horse Dance

Horse dancers are popular in Guntur district. Life size horse puppets are prepared with cattle-dung, hay and husk and coloured to look like real horses. These puppets are hollow in the middle, where the dancers -men and women- stand resembling riders on horse back.

In Guntur district, real horses are trained to dance according to the rhythm of the drums. Tinkling bells are tied to the fetlocks of the horse. During marriage processions and fairs the horse dance is a popular pass time in this district.

Karuva Dance

Karuva dance is popular in East Godavari district. Eight men dressed as Gopika's and eight dressed as Krishna's stand in a circle alternately. In the middle of the circle stand two more dancers dressed as Radha and Krishna. They dance to different rhymes. The movements in this dance are the most important. The gatis generally employed are chaturasara, Trisara and Misra.

The classical dance forms of Andhra Pradesh are mainly Kuchipudi and Bhamakalapam. They belong to the ancient school of Bharatnatyam. The temple dances and the court dances too have their own styles in Andhra.

Veethi Bhagavatam

Veethi Bhagavatam is a solo performance that originated from Kuchipudi tradition. The masters of Kuchipudi themselves thought of this new type and it evolved through women -artistes of courtesan families (Kalavantula) who were proficient in the solo dance -art of the Nautch.

The Kuchipudi tradition did not permit women to play female roles in its Bhagavata stories and the Nautch had its own repertoire of detached pieces and love songs. By crossing the features of these two, the form named Veethi Bhagavata or Gollakalapa was developed. The Veethi Bhagavata is performed during temple festivals, on occasions of marriage and other happy celebrations in the houses of rich patrons.

The Veethi Bhagavata has a single female artists, the main dancer, she supported by a secondary female artistes. The role of Vidhushaka is used to entertain and put across humour effectively in the play. He also add vehicle of wisdom. He is versatile and multi purpose character, the constant companion of the lady and also her chorist. It is its dialogue or argument in which the chief lady, representing a milkmaid (Golla), carries on with the Brahmin, that provides the Kalapam. She cross- examines the Brahmin as to his real Brahmin hood and expatiates on what a real Brahmin is according to the Sastras and under the torrent of her questions and Sanskrit quotation from the sastras, the poor Brahmin is left breathless.

The performance begins as with any traditional dance-drama. A curtain is held by two stage-hands and the main character performs behind it, her dance to the entrance song as sung by the chorus. The classic ragas of the Karnatik music are used in the songs, the Mridangam supplies the rhythmic accompaniment Jatis are orally recited and intricate rhythm patterns give the dancers footwork sufficient scope for artistry. She interprets the theme in the songs closely through Abhinaya.

3

Dances of Arunanchal Pradesh

The dances, performed by the tribes of Arunachal Pradesh, have been broadly divided into four groups. The first group is the ritual dances which may again be divided into five sub-groups. The first sub-groups includes those dances which form part of the various rituals performed to secure prosperity, good health and happiness of the dancer, his family, village or the whole community.

The second sub-group comprises of those dances performed in ceremonies related to agriculture and domestication of animals to secure a good harvest and increase of domestic animals respectively. The third sub-group is associated with the funeral ceremony when the soul is guided by a priest to its abode in the land of the dead and to prevent it from haunting its old residence. It is generally believed that if the soul returns to its old home the bereaved family suffers diseases and deaths.

The fourth sub-group consists of the fertility dances. These are magical in the sense that the imitation of the movements of coition is believed to promote fertility. War-dances make the fifth sub-group, which are on the decline with the stoppage of internecine feuds and raids. In the old days, when an expeditionary party was successful in killing an enemy or more, the victors used to perform a ceremony on return, so that the spirit of the slain could do no harm to the slayer. Only among the Idu Mishmis, the victim's family also used to perform rites praying for success in taking vengeance. Dance formed a part of this ceremony. The war-dance used to be prevalent among almost all the non-Buddhist tribes.

The second group is the festive-dance which forms the recreational part of a particular festival. The third group is the recreational dances which do not form part of any particular festival or ritual.

These are performed on occasions which inspire its participants to express their mirth through these dances. The fourth group is the pantomimes and dance-dramas which narrate a mythical story or illustrate a moral.

THE WANCHO DANCE

The Wancho tribes perform dances during appropriate occasions like festivals, ceremonies etc. Ozele festival of Wanchos is celebrated in February-March after the sowing of millet. It lasts for four days and was observed in Longkhau village. The dance is performed from about 9 p.m. to 11 p.m. inside the chief's house. Among the male-folk, boys, youths and adults take part while among women, only girls and those young married women who have not joined the husband's family, take part in the dance.

The dancers, dressed in their fineries, stand in a circle surrounding a bonfire. The girls stand on one side of the circle holding each other's hands. The male dancers hold a sword in the right hand and most of them place the left hand over the shoulder of the dancer to the left. The male dancers start singing when all take a short step with the right foot to the right, flex the knees with an accompanying forward swing of the sword and gently bring the left foot up to the heel of the right one.

They repeat this sequence of movements. When the singing of the male-dancers, end, which is generally on the eighth or ninth step, all stamp their right foot twice on the ground. The female dancers take up the singing in reply. They stamp the right foot twice on the ground during their turn of singing, once generally in the fourth step and the next at the end of the singing which generally falls on the ninth step. Again the male dancers take up the singing and thus the dance continues.

All the male dancers have a cane basket hanging at the waist over the buttocks. The basket is decorated with coloured straw tassels, monkey skulls or wild boar's tushes. The straw tassels of the baskets are decorated with coloured beads.

The straps of some of the baskets are decorated with white conch-shell discs. Each basket has a bell fitted at its bottom. The tinkling of so many bells is the only musical sound. All have anklets of straw and girdles of one or two loops of red cane or of bands of cowries or beads just below the knee. The boys and a few youths are naked but others wear a loin-cloth which is white or light blue in colour with two red stripes at the ends decorated with small beads of different colours.

This loin-cloth is tucked in position with a cane waist-band which is about six inches broad. The armlets are either of ivory, brass or red cane loops. The handle of the sword is decorated with coloured goat's hair. All wear some bead necklaces. Some wear necklaces of coins. The ear decorations are tufts of red woolen threads or ear-plugs decorated with the red seeds. Some have head-dresses made of bamboo, silver-shaped in a cone and decorated with horn-bill feathers. Some have red cane head-dresses decorated with wild boar's tushes.

The hair up to the middle of the crown is brought forward and cut so that the fringe reaches just up to the top of the fore-head while the hair of the back is kept long and tucked round a red or yellow coloured rectangular piece of wood, called the Kahpak. Some of these kahpak's are studded with small pieces of glass while some are decorated with carvings of the human figure or human skull or with a tuft of coloured goat's hair. The side of the head are shaven.

THE IDU MISHMI RITUAL DANCE

The Idu Mishmis have a ritual-dance and a fertility-dance. The ritual-dance is performed by the priest or priestess in the ceremonies of Ai-ah, Ai-him, Mesalah and Rren. The fertility-dance is performed on the last day of the Rren ceremony.

There is no definite myth about the origin of this ritual dance. According to local tradition, the first priest who officiated in a funeral ceremony was Chineuhu and his brother Ahihiuh, was the first priest who officiated in the other three ceremonies in which this dance forms a part. This dance is associated with the priestly office.

Besides the priest, there are three or four other dancers who are selected from amongst the spectators. In addition it is the usual dress which consists of a loin-cloth, a short-sleeved coat, and a sword slung on the right side, a leather bag slung on the left side and a few bead-necklaces, the priest wears a few other articles.

These articles are an apron with particular designs, a head-band decorated with two or three rows of cowries, a necklace studded with the teeth of tiger and bear and a few metal bells. A priestess wears these special articles in addition to the usual Mishmi woman's dress of a skirt, a long sleeved coat and bead-necklaces. The priestess is generally accompanied by female dancers. The accompanying dancers wear the usual dress.

The dancers stand in a line, the priest is second either from the right or left. During the dance, one dancer standing at one end of the line plays a small drum slung from his neck. The priest and the other two dancers play a very small semi-globular single-membrane drum, striking it with a bamboo-stick which is kept tied to the drum with a string. The fifth dancer, if any, plays a horn bugle.

When there are five dancers, the priest stands in the middle of the line. He sings a line of invocatory song while all the others play the musical instruments, flex the knees bobbing up and down and alternately raise the right and left heels and stamp these on the ground in time to the drum-beats. When the priest finishes singing the line, others repeat it in chorus. Again the priest sings another line of the song which the others repeat in chorus and thus it goes on.

After a prelude of flexing of knees and stamping of heels, they place one foot forward and immediately bring the other up beside it. If in the first step, the right foot is taken forward, then in the next step it is the left one. After each step, they flex the knees. Thus, they dance forward to the accompaniment of drumbeats and invocatory song. When they have danced forward for some distance, they dance backward with the same movement. Thus they dance moving forward and backward.

Sometimes they break away from the line formation and the four dancers standing in the four corners sing an invocatory song, play the musical instruments and dance flexing the knees and raising the right and left heel alternately and stamping these on the ground. Now and then they change positions dancing all the time but facing inward. Sometimes they dance in a circle following one another with tripping steps.

In another movement, they dance sideways either in a clockwise or anti-clockwise direction. They stand in a semi-circle and in the anti-clockwise movement, they take one step with the right foot to the right and immediately bring the left foot beside the right one. Thus they dance in a circle, flexing the knees after each step.

The priest does not demand any money for his priestly services, but the performer usually remunerates him according to his ability. The remuneration may also be paid in kind, e.g. with handloom coat, brass utensils or pigs.

THE IDU MISHMI RITUAL DANCE

The Idu Mishmis have a ritual-dance and a fertility-dance. The ritual-dance is performed by the priest or priestess in the ceremonies of Ai-ah, Ai-him, Mesalah and Rren. The fertility-dance is performed on the last day of the Rren ceremony.

There is no definite myth about the origin of this ritual dance. According to local tradition, the first priest who officiated in a funeral ceremony was Chineuhu and his brother Ahihiuh, was the first priest who officiated in the other three ceremonies in which this dance forms a part. This dance is associated with the priestly office.

Besides the priest, there are three or four other dancers who are selected from amongst the spectators. In addition it is the usual dress which consists of a loin-cloth, a short-sleeved coat, and a sword slung on the right side, a leather bag slung on the left side and a few bead-necklaces, the priest wears a few other articles. These articles are an apron with particular designs, a head-band decorated with two or three rows of cowries, a necklace studded with the teeth of tiger and bear and a few metal bells. A priestess wears these special articles in addition to the usual Mishmi woman's dress of a skirt, a long sleeved coat and bead-necklaces. The priestess is generally accompanied by female dancers. The accompanying dancers wear the usual dress.

The dancers stand in a line, the priest is second either from the right or left. During the dance, one dancer standing at one end of the line plays a small drum slung from his neck. The priest and the other two dancers play a very small semi-globular single-membrane drum, striking it with a bamboo-stick which is kept tied to the drum with a string. The fifth dancer, if any, plays a horn bugle.

When there are five dancers, the priest stands in the middle of the line. He sings a line of invocatory song while all the others play the musical instruments, flex the knees bobbing up and down and alternately raise the right and left heels and stamp these on the ground in time to the drum-beats. When the priest finishes singing the line, others repeat it in chorus. Again the priest sings another line of the song which the others repeat in chorus and thus it goes on.

After a prelude of flexing of knees and stamping of heels, they place one foot forward and immediately bring the other up beside it. If in the first step, the right foot is taken forward, then in the next step it is the left one. After each step, they flex the knees. Thus, they dance forward to the accompaniment of drumbeats and invocatory song. When they have danced forward for some distance, they dance backward with the same movement. Thus they dance moving forward and backward.

Sometimes they break away from the line formation and the four dancers standing in the four corners sing an invocatory song, play the musical instruments and dance flexing the knees and raising the right and left heel alternately and stamping these on the ground. Now and then they change positions dancing all the time but facing inward. Sometimes they dance in a circle following one another with tripping steps.

In another movement, they dance sideways either in a clockwise or anti-clockwise direction. They stand in a semi-circle and in the anti-clockwise movement, they take one step with the right foot to the right and immediately bring the left foot beside the right one. Thus they dance in a circle, flexing the knees after each step.

The priest does not demand any money for his priestly services, but the performer usually remunerates him according to his ability. The remuneration may also be paid in kind, e.g. with handloom coat, brass utensils or pigs.

Digaru Mishmi Buiya Dance

The Digaru Mishmis have two types of dances called Buiya and Nuiya. The Buiya dance has two types of movements and it is performed for entertainment while the Nuiya is a ritual-dance performed by a priest.

Buiya dance is performed on any festive occasion like the Duiya, Tazampu and Tanuya festivals which are performed for the prosperity and good health of the performer and his household. This dance may also performed after a feast arranged by a family to entertain the fellow villagers who co-operate with it opening a new field.

The dance is performed in the passage which runs along one side of the house from the front to the rear. Men and women take part in this dance. There is no limit to the age of the dancers although generally children and old persons do not take active part in the dance itself but merely sit by, as spectators.

There is no special costume for this dance, so they perform this dance wearing their usual dress. The male dancer wears a loin-cloth a sleeveless jacket, a turban and ear-rings. The female dancer wears a blouse, a long skirt reaching down to the ankle with a short one wrapped over it and a side-bag on the left side. They wear necklaces, large silver-ear-plugs and a silver fillet with its strap studded with coins or cowries.

The dancers stand in a line, one behind the other, in the passage. One of the dancers plays a drum while another plays a gong. Cymbals are played, if available, by another dancer. Keeping time to the beats of the drum, gong and cymbals, the dancers take one step forward with the right foot, then gently bring the left foot up to the heel of the left one flexing the knees as before.

They dance forward repeating this sequence of movements till they reach the rear of the passage with the same sequence of movements. Thus they dance up and down the passage of the house. They may or may not sing to the accompaniment of the dance. When they sing a song, it may be solo or in chorus. There is another movement when they dance with skipping steps but with no accompanying song. The skipping steps of the female-dancers are lower and graceful while those of the male-dancers are higher and more vigorous.

The dancers get no remuneration. There is no formal training but they learn the dance movements by imitating those of the elders.

THE KHAMPTI DANCE

The Kamptis, who are Buddhists, have many dance-dramas through which they unfold some stories or depict mythical events bearing ethical lessons. These dramas are generally staged during the religious festivals of Potwah, Sankian or Khamsang, constituting the entertainment part of the festivals.

The dance is called ka and the dance-drama is called kapung (ka-dance; pung-story) and actually means a story depicted through the dance. The rehearsal of a drama starts about one month before a festival. This may be done in the monastery or in any house of their choice. The well-to-do-villagers invite the drama-party when the drama is staged in the front courtyard or in some suitable open space near their house.

Women do not take part in the drama. The female role, if any, is played by a man in woman's costume. After the performances, the party is given a remuneration of seven, fourteen, twenty-eight or forty-two rupees-always an amount divisible by seven. They purchase with this money the costumes and masks used in the dramas. The surpluses, if any, is shared by the members of the drama party.

Ka Fifai Dance-Drama

The Ka Fifai drama is woven round the theme of the traditional belief that ghosts appear and kidnap girls or men and trouble them. The participants in the drama consist of a man, his daughter who is kidnapped, the ghost who does the kidnapping, the Ministers of the State who make preparations for war against the ghost, the King of the stage in which the girl's father is a subject, and the king's men who go out to capture the ghost.

The drama opens with a man and his daughter walking in the garden. The ghost appears and captures the girl, and immediately the man greatly aggrieved rushes to the king's court to inform him of the incident and beseech him the rescue his daughter. The king's anger is aroused at this news and he calls for his Ministers and asks them to prepare for war. The King's men go in search of the ghost and bring him before the king, who severely warns him never to do such a thing again. The ghost frightened bows before the king and with this ends the drama.

Ponung Dance (Adis)

Adi village has a rich cultural life. The tribal people are famous for their Ponung that is dancing with the accompaniment of songs. A group of girls dance in a circle holding each other by stretching their hands over each others shoulders while the leader-usually a man called the Miri-dances and sings in the centre-holding aloft and shaking a sword like musical instrument called 'Yoksha'. First he sings a line and then it is repeated in chorus by the maidens rhythmically in circle at a low pace. On all important occasions ponung is arranged.

SadinukTSo (Akas)

The Akas have a number of dances and songs for the different socio-religious festivities. One of the well known dance among the Akas is the Sadinuktso. A member from the boy's group comes forward, gives his performance for a short while and recedes. A girl then comes and she also dances all alone. This relation goes on till all the boys and girls of the group have danced. No song is sung with this dance. It is generally performed in marriages, guest, entertainments or on the construction of a new house.

4

Tribal Dances of Assam

HUSARI AND BIHUNAS

The two main forms of dancing are Husari and Bihunas.

Husari is carol singing. Batches of boys and young men led by older men go from house to house, sing and dance in the front or back courtyard and collect subscriptions to be spent on repairing the village Namghar (community centre) and on feasting. The dance commences with singing of hymns led by a comparatively elder person. The music is staccato. Each dance lasts only a minute or two. Husari is more religious than festive and gives clear indications of the origin of the Bihu festival in some ancient fertility cult.

Bihu songs and dances invariably follow the main item of Husari singing which consists of specially composed songs of religious themes sung by members of the party moving in a circle. These songs have a wide range of folk-tunes and are sung in praise of the great festival with the music of accompanying drums and various bamboo instruments.

It is a dance of youth and of the spirit of spring, it expresses an exuberant spirit, like a Bihu song, it tends to express the erotic sentiment more than anything else. The Bihu drummer, often utters his bols and follows their reproduction on his drum, and then dances in such a way that he appears to have no bones in his body at all.

Dhuliya and Bhawariya

Generally accompanying bhawuas, i.e. theatrical performances of the type of miracle plays of Europe in the middle ages. These dances verging on acrobatics are performed to tunes of vigorous music provided with drums and cymbals. Masks are sometimes used.

Deodhani

This dance form is associated with the worship of the snake goddess Manasa. A Deodhani girl, in a trance like inspired state, goes on dancing to the accompaniment of Kham (drum) and Ciphung (flute) propitiating many a deity beginning with Siva and ending with Lakshmi, she at one stage takes a sword and a shield and performs a virile war-dance.

Zikirs

Zikirs are songs sung by Assamese Muslims to the accompaniment of dancing in circles and clapping of hands.

Mohauhau or Mahkheda

It is also considered as a festival. In Kamrup district on a full moon night in Nov-Dec, boys in groups go from house to house and sing and dance, striking the ground with bamboo sticks and taking leaps and turns. The ceremony is believed to be helpful in driving away mosquitoes.

Apsara-Sabah

This is a ceremony in which the nymphs of the air are invoked during calamities and lean times, women with flowing hair dance in circles. The rhythm is provided by striking bamboo sticks on conch-shells or bangles.

5

Tribal Dances of Bihar

FOLK MUSIC

Folk songs are mostly sung by Bihari amateurs all over the state. The Thumar or Barahmasa is sung by female in groups when they are engaged in paddy plantation. When grinding corn in Jata or Chakki, they sing Jatusari. Sohar is sung on the occasion of child-birth and Sumangali, when marriage rites are to conclude.

In early nineteenth century Bihar, music was cultivated by certain professional classes alone and rich men extended generous patronage to musicians, especially to superior female artistes who were allowed small endowments.

The Hindu Kathaks went about in-groups of three or four and sang with Tamburu, Sarangi, Majira and dholak accompaniment, mostly from Jaideva's 'Geet Govinda'. They sang common songs and love songs of Bengal.

The Yajaks were employed at funerals, the Bhajaniyas and Kirtaniyas were employed by Brahmans to sing holy songs after the morning prayer, Roshan Chouki parties were employed to play on pipes and drums and also to accompany Muharram processions.

The Pamarias, men and women, who were mostly Muslims, thronged to sing where marriages were being held and birth has taken place and were satisfied only when they were given a handsome remuneration. Most women sang at marriage ceremonies.

There was also a class of dancing boys called Bhakliyas. These dancers had no fixed abode. They came to Bihar to celebrate Holy in the month of Chaitra.

Folk Dances

The folk dance tradition in Bihar has three distinct streams. One of them is the folk dances of Videha, the present Mithila which is mainly rooted in the songs of poets, the second stream is those of the Adivasis which are closer to nature, social institutions and rituals. The third stream relates to the Chhau dance of Seraikella and other regions of south Bihar.

The folk dances of Mithila are religious, social or sectarian. In the religious type, gods and goddesses are invoked through dance, performed to the rhythm of folk songs and such musical instruments as the dhol, pipahi, pakhwaf, and danka. The Ram-leela nach, Bhagat nach, Kirtaniya nach, Kunjvawt nach, Naradi nach, Vdypat nach and puja Arti nach are all religious folk dances of Mithila.

Folk dances for men are accompanied by songs and musical instruments and the footwork of the dancers is in tune with the swar and tal of the music. The dances exclusively for women are Jhijhiya nach, Jatajutia nach, Sama Chawka nach. The only mixed group dance is Saturi dance of Mithila. In the family dance called Bakho nach, the husband and wife participate on the occasion of the birth of a child or a similar joyous occasion. The different lower-caste groups have their own exclusive dances such as Chamar natua, Kanala mai nach, Dampha-Basuli nach. There are such popular dances as Pamariya nach, Videshia nach and Kathputli nach.

Chhau Dance

This is a folk dance of Seraikella Kharsawam region. The word Chhau signifies a mask. Originally a war dance to perfect fighting techniques, it has over the years evolved into a narrative ballet. The dancer's identity and sex are concealed on account of the mask he wears when performing the Chhau. On the eve of the spring festival, every year, people in Seraikella celebrate with the colourful show of 'Chhau' performance. The Seraikella royalty preserves, projects and participates in Chhau, in the month of Chaitra Paru, April in the venue of the kings palace.

The Adivasi version of the Chhau is called Sastriya Nritya. In the performance of Sastriya Nritya, the dancers sometimes do not use the mask. The use of songs, a common feature of all folk dances is wholly absent in the Chhau. The dancer expresses mood or theme through the medium of varied gestures, all of the exquisite artistic appeal to the accompaniment of the veena, flute, drum. All there folk dances have their roots in the traditions of the region in the past.

TRIBAL FOLK DANCES

Music and dance play a pivotal role in the life of the tribal communities. Most of them have well-organised institutions for providing training in these arts to young men and women. In a large part of the tribal area of the state have youth dormitories where regular instruction in dance and music is imparted every morning.

Most tribal groups have exquisite folk songs dealing with different themes and suited to different occasions. In most tribal communities there are special dances for different festivals and these dances are highly enchanting. To the tribals, music and dance are not a sort of recreation. They are so closely interwoven with tribal courtship that they have often been described as an expression of stylised animality.

Young men and women meet freely in the dancing ground of their village, forgetting all their sorrows and sufferings. They give themselves away to singing and dancing. Ladem with themes of tender of love, their songs have highly seductive charm. The dancing ground is not merely a place of recreation or training in music and dance but a rendezvous for court ship.

To the Adivasis of south Bihar, dance is very breath of life rather than a means of amusement. Their songs are generally accompanied by dances. They will change according to the seasons. They have their dancing platform, often under the shade of a big tree. The Santhals are born singers and dancers. Their important dance festivals are Maghi parva, Dasia parva, Ba parva and Karma. The Birhors, Hos and Kisans have their special choreography expressive of their culture and art traditions.

The Oraons and Mundas have their dances. They are Jadur, Karma and Jatra dances. The Karma is the most important festival among these tribes. On the eleventh day of Bhadra they plant the branch of Karma tree quite ceremoniously and then after worshipping it, men and women dance. The entire village community filled with high spirits, dances continuously for three days. After the rains they perform the Jatra dance. The paika dance is inextricably mated to Munda culture and it is performed on the occasion of a marriage. This is a mock-fight dance with swords and shields meant only for men folk. The Jadur is performed on the occasion of the Sarhul festival in April.

The Karma festival is also celebrated by the Mathos, Harijans, Napits, Mandals. Their womenfolk dance round the Karma plant.

The Nachni and Natua dances are semi-professional. The Nachni and her Rasik dance to the tune of the shehnai, magara etc. holding handkerchiefs in their hands and wish sashes tied round their waists, two male accompanists sing and clap. The Nachni performs her dance on different joyous occasions and seasons.

Her singing and dancing go together. Her song is sung in the pach-parganiya dialect. It is a mixture of Hindu and Kurmali. At Silli, a town-let in the Ranchi district, all Nachnis and Rasiks gather together and perform the Rasa on the Kartik purnima day. The Natua dance is essentially a duet. The performers dancing to the accompaniment of the dhol, shehnai and Nagara.

6

Tribal Dances of Goa

Mussoll

Mussoll is a folk-play-cum-dance played by the Kshatriyas among the Christians from the two hamlets of Chandor-Kott and Kouddi in Chandor village. Mussoll in Konkani, is an instrument used by women folk for pounding rice. It is a dance based on the legendry powers of the ancient Kshatriyas. This play must have been exhibited at the sabha-mandapa (assembly- hall) of the royal temple of Lord Chareshwar (moon god), with as many variations as circumstances of the time permitted. It is also called 'Musllam-Fell' or Khell. The dance is a war dance - a dance of a martial race or caste.

From the wording of the song, the Mussoll dance commemorates the victory of King Harihara II, son of Bukka I of the Vijayanagar empire, over the Cholas at the ancient fort of Chandrapur around 1310AD. King Harihara is supposed to have claimed descent from the lunar race. Mussoll dance has a constituent symbol, i.e. a bear which is the symbol of Cholas.

Originally the dance was held on the full moon night in the month of Phalguna. Now it is held on the second night of the Christian carnival. The preparation for the dance-cum-play commence on the first day of the carnival (i.e. Sunday). One of the most senior Gaunkars (Kshatriya or Chaddho) is eligible to become the captor of the bear. Dressed in ancient native costumes consisting of a Dhoti, over which he wears a white shirt like garment, a jacket and a turban and anklets on the left foot, he carries a rope in his hand and a ghumatt (which is a local percussion instrument in Goa consisting of goat-skin taut over the mouth of an earthen pot, of which the other mouth is kept open) slung down his neck.

Another Gaunkar dressed in a ragged black blanket, his face covered with a mask of a bear, a rope tied round his waist, the end of which is in the hands of the captor and carrying a branch of a mango or 'rumbodd' tree is taken prisoner by the captor, and exhibited to the Kshatriya households in the Kott area of Chandor.

Next day at six o'clock in the morning, both the captor and the captive bear proceed to the main gate of the Fort near San Tiagos Chapel (St. James). They come from the gate, the captor beating the ghumatt and the bear growling out, to the entrance of the chapel. There the captive bear, deposits the branch of the tree to signify total surrender.

From there, they go along from house to house of the Gaunkars, care being taken to arrive last at the house of the captor where he and the captive bear change into their normal vestments and disband from there.

On the second day of the Carnival, at about 10 in the night, all Gaunkars assemble at the Sabha-mandapa of the temple of Lord Chandreshwar. A short Christian prayer is said and then the dance can begin at the Mandd which is a place, marked for communal festive functions. When they have finished dancing, the procession led by torch bearers and attendants proceeds to the Chapel of San Tiago near the main gate of the Fort, where they dance for a while. Then they go from house to house of every Gaunkar and after the last house has been visited, they return to the 'Mandd' and disband. At every dwelling, the lady of the house must welcome the dancers by bringing out a lamp.

On the third day of the Carnival, at about ten in the morning, one Gaunkar dressed in the native costume and carrying a ghumatt and accompanied by a peasant woman who carries with her a basket of cow dung, a pot of water and a broom, takes the same route of the previous night, dance and sees that the barik rounnem (which is the central spot where the Mussoll was beaten hard into the ground during the dance) is levelled and cow dunged to signify the return of peace and to reassure prosperity and well being of the city inhabitants. A token coin is given to the sweeper-woman and another one to the Gaunkar as the households contribution to the Mandd fund. This fund serves to meet the incidental expenses of the dance performance and miscellaneous activities.

The Mussoll or pounding pestle used in the dance is made of solid bamboo of about 6-7 feet in length with inserted hawk's bells and is carried only by those who will actually dance. The torches are made of coconut, sliced mid-way longitudinally dried like copra and treated with a mixture of mud and cow dung. These were held upright on a spike at the end of a long bamboo stick. A wick was inserted, which burns under the oil that oozes out of the dried Kernel of the coconut. Besides these, torches of wax or of dried coconut-tree leaves will be used.

The dance consist of a march and the beating of the barik rounnem. The march has a martial beat and has three different steps. First a combination of clockwise and anti-clockwise full turns. Second a serpentine forward movement done in half turns, left and right and third as a straight march on the ball of the feet.

The starting step is always with the left foot, except that in the first step whilst the left side dancers are completing the full turn starting with the left foot. The right dancers do the same starting with the right foot in order to keep the movement either clockwise or anti-clockwise.

The dance has only two beats : single beat and a triple time beat. The steps are basically a one-step and a three-step movement. But a combination of one-step, two steFp and three step movements each in clockwise and anti-clockwise turns is usually danced. The dance always starts with the left foot forward and in an anti-clockwise circular direction.

The most enchanting is the twirl in which every alternate dancer leaves the ring or the barik rounnem and they form together an outer ring dancing in an opposite direction in three-step movements, while the dancers in the inner circle barik-rounnem do the three-step movement in full turns. Though the original song of the Mussoll dance is on an eastern melody, it is weighed down by western music with the Portuguese impact on it.

Manddo is a song or rather a poignant story of love told in the form of a lovely song. The word Manddo, derives from the Sanskrit 'mandalam' meaning circular movement. It is believed that originally the Konkani Manddo dance involved movement in circle. At present such circular patterns are noticed when the dancers get into a feverish pitch in the concluding stages of the dance.

In the normal course the dance moves along parallel lines, with graceful movements to and fro, advancing and reading, the men displaying in a flourish towards the women their colourful handkerchiefs and the women admiring their toy fans, with an eye on the men.

The Manddo music appears to have been strongly influenced by Latin or rather Italian music. The dance-song Manddo may be called a synthesis of the Italian minuet and the temple Devadasi dance-song.

The singing moves majestically in a slow, andante rhythm, with dignity and grace. It falls into a drowsy dormant mood towards the fag-end of the singing function when the singers are tired and may have imbibed considerable quantities of alcohol and cannot go on much longer. The Manddo has attained the virtual status of a classical or art song after being subjected to a process of sophistication and stylisation. The ghumott provided the right beat, attuned as it is to Manddo singing and dance. The beat of it moves faster and faster as the singing progresses to a crescendo, on to a frenzy and conclusion.

Though the Manddo is a story of love told in song, there have been a few songs composed on a similar pattern but involving themes of a political nature called Political Manddo. There are Manddos on the revolts and uprisings of the Ranes, the legendary Warriors of the Sattari taluka of Goa, and the Christian Kustoba's feats of daring against the Portuguese government etc.

Every year a Manddo festival is held as an event of importance from 1966 onwards, with a special Bernardo Award for the best Manddo.

The Dulpod Or Durpod

If the Manddo can be called an expression of the romantic aspect of the Goan, the Dulpod that follow it is the singing repertoire. The Durpod gives its couplets a compressed and catchy note providing fleeting glimpses of the variety of Goan life. It is a thing of joy and gaiety, evoking laughter, carefree in its mood and lively in its expression.

As the hunting melody of the Manddo moves towards a conclusion and ends, it is followed by the Dulpod, the beat of which is the opposite to that of the Manddo and more quick-moving, symbolising the lively sprightliness of life among the common folk. The Dulpod moves into a staccato beat and quickens in a syncopated rhythm.

The most popular among the Dulpods are the one about Cecila and her sewing, Modgonvam Thovyanger and 'Maya-ya-ya' or Lia-lia-lo. The Dulpod encompasses the whole of life in its infinite variety- human, animal and vegetables. All of it is captured in the Dulpod in couplets, whose effect in its wording, is very pithy and telling.

Deknni or Dakhnni

It is a form of song-cum-dance in the Christian repertoire of song among the people of Goa. It is a song composed by

Christian artistes perhaps an expression of the Goan Christian nostalgia for their lost Hindu past, where the Devadasi or kolvont in Konkani was an alluring symbol.

The term Dakhnni in Sanskrit means devil of a female. It is danced in a manner that verges on the voluptuous, with gyrations and significant gestures which are so suggestive in character. The main danseuse is joined by other females, enticing in their appearance, who announce themselves to the audience.

Then begins the pleading and coaxing by the women, including finally the boatman with offerings of anklets, bracelets, nose-ringlets, by turns and finally clinching the deal with the offer of a kiss, which latter the boatman accepts in the surrender to their wiles, to ferry them across to the other side of the river to a place belonging to a man called Damu, where they have to perform at the wedding.

Kunnbi-Geet

Kunnbi-geet is a folk song prevalent among the hardy labourers called Kunnbis which are sung to the accompaniment of the ghumatt and the drum and the clang of cymbals. These Kunnbis are found concentrated in the Chandor-Kouddi hamlet of Chandor in an exclusive ward of their own called Kunbeam-Vaddo now being called by them as Miream-Jirem.

The theme of their songs varies from romantic love to bitter resentment and satire couched in suggestive language against their landlords (Bhakar) who have usurped their lands and are exploiting them. The Kunnbis sing songs at different times, like at different stages of cultivation of rice. It is done at the time of Nondnni (weeding), Mollnni (threshing), Luvnni (harvesting). Winnowing does not find expression in songs. There are also songs with reference to the rain and its bounty.

Occupational Songs Amon

The Goan fisherman have their own folk-songs which

they sing at the time of the Sangodd (two boats being tied together). The most famous of these performances being at Calangute, at the time of their first trips to the sea after the resumption of the fishing seasons after monsoons.

The toddy-tappers who are the largest group among the Sudir group of castes in Chandor, have their own charming songs called Rendrachim Geetam (songs of toddy tappers), which are equally fully of native verve. Other occupational songs are the Mitta-geet of salt pan workers and the Ghanno of the oil-mill crushers.

The general run of workers/labourers have another type of song sung at random at siesta time or may be during recreational hours, to the accompaniment of ghumatt and Kansallim (cymbals) which are known as tandnni which is derived from 'tan' (thirst). Such songs arise from the native soil have the freshness and smell of it.

Konkani songs of Goa are found in an infinite variety. For the song has been the mainstay of the Goan in his hour of joy and sorrow, even in the expressions of protest against injustice and oppression even when he was confronted with the threat of extermination.

The cradle songs in Goa are known as Painno or Halloio. Though they are very few in number, they are fine expressions of lilting tunes, the best of the existing ones being Painnem Halounk (to rock the cradle) and Dol re Baba (Rock, baby).

There are songs for various ceremonies connected with weddings. After the engagement is over, Goan Christians and Hindus follow more or less similar customs in their weddings. The songs that accompany the different stages and ceremonies of the wedding ritual are called Zoti.

Another lilting traditional song, sings of the cowherds and milkmaids who used to come down from the Ghats in search of plenty, in Goa and the regions around it. The song is sung alternately by choruses of two groups, boys and girls.

Talgoddi Dance

There are some activities which are peculiar to Goan Hindus. The spirit of the carnival finds its expression in Chandor village among the Hindus in the form of the Talgoddi dance. It literally means young men in rhythm in Konkani. It has eight distinct modes, expressed through its theme and is danced by eight to twelve men.

They show their skill in footwork and muscles by dancing a number of group dances, which are a spontaneous outburst of genuine folk spirit, on the Mandd or paved courtyard under the graceful and cool mattov (pavilion made of thatched green coconut, tree plaited leaves and mounted on betel nut poles). It is a sort of an aimless dance expressing a pure rhythmic pattern of human movements, energy and sheer joy of living.

Shigmo

Shigmo or Shimga is the Goan expression of the sprit of spring around the month of March, very close to the carnival. The focal hour of its celebration is the full moon day of the month of Phalguna. Shigmo is the time for the home coming of the brave, who had left their firesides with the Dussehra.

For the farmer and the shepherd, it is the time of rebirth of nature and for the warriors, the time of return of man. Ceremonial thanksgiving, processions to temples and shrines, songs, dramas and dances, bonfires, masquerades and abuses, festoons, banners, colours and sweets are in plenty on this occasion.

Rang-panchami gets merged into the celebration with the throwing of colours in a boisterous manifestation of gaiety.

The other manifestations of Shigmo in Goa are the Romatt or Mell, Goff and Tonnya Mell, Dashavatari Khell and Kalo plays and dances. These are performed in most of the rural areas of Goa where Hindus predominate.

Foogddi

It is a dance very much loved among Goan Hindu girls and women. The details of the dance vary from caste to caste in Goa. Brahmin girls dance it with a brass pot on the head. Farmers, fisher folk and Kunnbis (Gavddis) dance it by forming an interlocked circle often of up to 12 girls. The Mahar women of Pednem area, dance it singly throughout, though in a group with exquisite footwork and attractive rhythm, which is kept up with foot claps every time the dancer revolves around herself.

At the Chovoth in Goa, nature revives the spirit of fulfillment with the season of fruitfulness. An uncontrollable explosion of energy sets the feet in motion. The girls and women start singing and dancing before Lord Ganesha. The most popular form of Foogddi in Goa is the one with circle formation which begins with the chanting of religious invocations. Konkani songs of special significance as well as of social themes follow upon the religious hymns.

They are sung by first improvising some homely group activity like grinding, washing or kneading which provides them with a dramatic setting. In this conductive setting, the group exchanges opinions and information in crisp couplet and salacious stanzas. It can also include scandals and gossip about those who are absent from the scene.

After this first part in slow tempo, the group breaks up into pairs and with interlocked hands, swirls around with gradually increasing pace, singing songs of matching speed. When the swirling attains maximum speed, they simply keep up the rhythm by blowing air through the mouth, making Foo.. Foo sounds.

When totally exhausted after the song and dance they sink down with heady satisfaction, laughing yet looking jealously at the pairs still spinning like tops with the dizzy emissions of Foo..Foo..Foo.. in the air. This unique sound in the expression of the song has bestowed the name of Foogddi, on the dance form. Foogddi is an all weather indoor dance and needs no special religious occasion for performances. It is mostly danced on all important religious and social occasions. It may even form the tail-end portion of other dance forms like the "Dhalo".

Dhalo

This song-cum-dance is also an all women affair like the 'foogddi'. The language of the song is Konkani with a slight admixture of Marathi. Dhalo are played (khellttat) rather than danced (nachtat). They are played out on the moonlit winter nights in the courtyard of the house. They are slower in tempo, songs prevailing predominantly over the movements. The front yard of the house, where normally the newly harvested corn (paddy) is processed, is dug and paved carefully and later plastered with cow dung almost to a cement like finish.

After the rice grains are winnowed, dried and stored, this paved place serves as a venue for all the socio-cultural activities of the village. There is a specific spot close to the door step called a Mandd or station. Here every activity is initiated with a puja and a lamp lit. This spot is considered sacred and represents the spirit of the occasion. The courtyard is later covered with a canopy of woven coconut-tree leaves, supported by a framework of betel-nut-tree poles. This covering over the Mandd is called Mattov in konkani.

Participants start gathering in the courtyard by 9 PM on the moonlit night of the Pausha month, according to the Hindu calendar. As many as 24 women take part in each session of this dance-cum-song affair. They split up into two parallel rows of 12 each, facing each other and form a close-knit unit by linking themselves with arm-around the back arrangement, singing in unison. They sway, bend, move forward and backwards, singing songs of religious and social importance, unhappy and sad things of old, which are locally composed from memory and revised extempore with addition or change of words and lines here and there to suit the occasion. The liveliest fun of a Dhalo session, occurs on the concluding day. The week which can be called women's lib week concludes with a sense of freedom. Therein women put on, all sorts of dresses of a fancy variety including those of various male roles, those of animals and birds and act out their respective parts and fantasies meticulously and with great dramatic gusto.

Ovi Songs

The Ovi songs relating to ceremonies of a profane nature like weddings etc are very much current in Goa among the Hindus, while they have almost disappeared among the Christians with few exceptions. They are sung by women while applying the coconut-pulp milk to the bride and groom, while preparing condiments for dinners etc. The most popular are those that concern with the spirit of fertility in the biblical terms of increase and multiply.

When the missionaries first began their work of spreading of Christianity in Goa, they made use of the existing Konkani metres, the main one used by them being the Ovi. People would gather around a fire or a cross and reverently sing Ovis composed by the missionaries in Konkani using biblical themes and other religious symbols.

Dantear Ovio meaning those ovis which are sung while grinding wheat and rice for various food preparations on the hand-mill (dantem in konkani) at wedding time, are sung in Goa. As the women grind, they crush their worries and sorrows in a symbolical gesture. The best of these ovis are found in the villages of Savoi-Verem, Boma and Zambaulin.

7

Tribal Dances of Gujarat

The sun temple at Modhera in Mehsana district (102 km from Ahmedabad, capital city of Gujarat), in north Gujarat, built during the reign of the Solanki king Bhimdev I, represents one of the most magnificent monuments of Gujarat. The temple, though in ruins, is considered one of the best specimens of Indian art and architecture of the by gone era. The temple dedicated to Lord Surya, the sun god has its outer walls covered with sculptures in which the figures of Lord Surya are prominent.

The beautiful Sun Temple acts as the backdrop during the festival of Indian classical dances held every year in January for three days. This annual festival of dance is organized by the Tourism Corporation of Gujarat. The idea is to present classical dance forms in an atmosphere they were originally presented in.

8

Tribal Dances of Haryana

Ras Leela

This dance is common among the people living in the Braja area of the Faridabad district. Lord Vishnu has been manifest in many incarnations. He is the supreme embodiment. He is Lord Krishna. The Gopis of Braj Bhoomi, the simple milk maid are his true devotees. Krishna choose them as the finest examples of human beings. Radha, the most beautiful of the Gopis, proud of her beauty and power over men was the last one to surrender to the utter bliss of the lord. Ras Leela becomes a dance of spiritual ecstasy with God pervading the world as his own self and as the selves of the dancing gopis. The gopis form a circle around a Krishna. In this circular dance the bracelets,anklets and the bells of the gopis sound together in perfect harmony. Gopis moving in Rhythm, sway their bodies gracefully.

Phag Dance or Phalgun or "Faag" Dance

This is a seasonal dance,through which agricultural people express their joy and vigour. During the month of February -March,they have a little leisure between sowing and harvesting. The crops are growing well, the spring is on and the rural folk express themselves through song and dance.

In this dance men and women group together. The rhythm takes them on to emotional expression through their hands, eyes, and feet. The dance involves a variety of movement,requiring sound co-ordination. Women wear traditional costumes in different colours. Men similarly display different colours in their turbans. They sing in the ancient Daamal style, a combination of dance and song, the origin of which dates to the hoary past, it is a mixed dance but some times it is performed by men only. The songs are different in each case.

Daph dance

Daph dance is also a seasonal dance connected with the harvest and spring. It depicts the joyful emotions of the farmers. Men and women of all sections of the village community participate in this dance, separately. For melodic instruments the ancient Haryanavis used flutes, lutes and beens. The daph used in this dance is an ancient instrument. The songs are most suited to the occasion. The sound of the ornaments worn by the women also becomes a part of the dance-orchestra.

Dhamal Dance

Dhamal dance is as old as the Mahabharatha. It is popular among the Ahirs of Gurgaon district. It is also in vogue in Mahendargarh and Jhajjar. The dance is rooted in the deeper emotions of the people, is performed on moonlit nights of Phalgun. When the winter veil of fog and mist is lifted from the face of the earth and whisper of spring is in the air indeed. The dancers assemble in an open space and form themselves into a circle. They start with a song to the sound of Dhamal beats. The songs sung during the dance relate to the burden of love and labour. They depict the villager's hopes, aspirations, their love -longings and joys and sorrows. Between fifteen and twenty dancers participate in the dance. Old musical instruments like Sarangi, Been, Dholak and Khartals constitute the orchestra. First of all the orchestra men make a line and start playing folk tunes. The dancers move in front of them emerging right and left when the dance starts.

Loor

Loor is a well known dance of Haryana. It is performed around the Holi festival and is very popular in the Bangar and Bagar parts of the region. In the Dadri area the term Loor is used for a girl. The participants in this dance are all girls. The dancers stand in two rows facing each other, in the form of a semi circle. One party starts a song. The burden of the song being

"Your bahu has given birth to a daughter and a son is born on this side, why not marry the two".

The dance starts with this song. For quite a while they discuss this problem. Finally the proposal is accepted. The next topic is about the presents to be given by the parents of the son to the girl at the time of marriage.

Marriage itself is performed through the dance. The girl has reached her sasural or in-laws place. There will be full of sentiment. She mourns in song and dance. The husband is away in the army and not expected back for another twelve years.

The unhappy girl addresses an imaginary pigeon and through a song she persuades the pigeon to convey her message to her husband. She continues her song and dance till the pigeon returns and sits on her shoulder. The pigeon informs her that her husband is coming home soon. With this message her joy know no bounds. The rhythm and tempo of her song now increase. Her companions who have come to congratulate her, circle around her and take the dance to its climax.

Gugga dance

Gugga Pir has several names :-Guru Gugga, Zahir Pir and Bagarwalla. Gugga is worshipped practically all over Haryana and devotees are scattered over the neighbouring states of Rajasthan, Punjab and Himachal.

The Pir was born on Bhadon Naumi at Dadreva village in Bikaner (Rajasthan). The day is celebrated as Gugga

Naumi allover northern India. Gugga is said to be a Chauhan Rajput. Colonel Tod is of the view that his name was Bachraj. According to a folk legend he was married to Kumari Sirial, daughter of Raja Sanjha of Kamrup He is equally worshipped by both Hindus and Muslims. About a week or two Before Gugga Naumi, his devotees take out a procession, led by a bhagat,carrying Gugga Kichhari.

It is a strong and long bamboo stick decorated with fans, garlands, flowers and coloured pieces of cloth.Five Bhagats are the Main dancers. They carry their own musical instruments in their hands, consisting of Dholak, Manjiras, Deru (a small side drum), Chimta and Cymbals. The bhagats sing a song in praise of Gugga.

The dance is very simple. The dancers feet move according to the rhythm or their songs. As the tempo increases, they shed tears and beat their chests with iron chains.

These parties are seen coming in Haryana villagers during the month of Bhadon. It is an exclusively male dance and falls in the category of ritualistic dances. It create an atmosphere charged with spiritual fervour among the devotees of Gugga.

Jhumar dance

This dance takes in the name from Jhumar, an ornament commonly worn on the fore head by young married girls. It is performed exclusively by women. They form a circle and move gracefully, accompanied by the beats of dholak and Thali. There are many variations each with its own distinctive rhythm. The dancers loose themselves in gay abandon, dressed in colourful costumes.

The performance lasts several hours. A girl comes forwards and breaks in to song. When girl sing the song, another girl then steps forward, swaying rhythmically with perfect poise. The second line of the song is shared by both. The tempo increases as the dance proceeds. The other girl do not leave their places but keep on singing the song and clapping their hands against each other. There is a short pause before a new line of the song is started.

This dance resembles the well-known Punjabi Gidda and is thus named Haryanic Gidda. It is common in all parts of the state.

Ghumar Dance

Some dancers receive their inspiration from religion. The gods and the elements are invoked to shower their blessing on the labours of a community.

Ghumar is a Rajasthani dance but it is popular in Laharu, Dadri and some parts of the Hissar and Bhiwani, bordering Rajasthan. The dance is performed by women devotees on their way to the temple. Young women and girls carrying brass plates of offerings in their hands go to the temple singing devotional songs. The dance is performed on Diwali, the festival of lights and Holi, the festivals of spring or on the occasion of the local ceremony of Gangor Puja.

Brass plates in their hands, girls make a circle and start singing. The Musicians strike a chord and as soon as the tune begins to take shape and gain momentum, the dancers put their offerings aside forming a large circle and dances gracefully with uplifted arms to the simplest beats. Slowly the dance gather momentum, the swaying bodies become frantic, taking the dance to its climax.

Khoria Dance

This dance is a variety of Jhumar dance. It is performed by woman only. It is popular in the central areas of Haryana. It is connected with the daily life of the people and with the most important events like harvest. Singing a folk song, the girls enter dancing place and make a ring. The simple movements acquire form and colour with the swirling off their full-gold-work skirts and coloured chundries and the gleam and jingle of heavy rustic jewellery.

The graceful steps give place to faster tempo until two or three pairs of the girls break from the ring into the centre with crossed arms joined together swirling on the axis of their feet. The girls in the ring clap to the beat of the drum. In final stage the dance is around the circumference.

Holi Dance

This exuberant dance is connected with the seasonal festival of spring. When the rural community rejoices and relaxes after the completion of their agricultural operations. It is performed in various formations to the accompaniment of drums and pipes.

Both men and women participate in this dance. Percussion instruments like dhol, jhajh, chimta, khartal and thalis and anklets on the feet of the dancers produce the rhythm. Abir, gulal and coloured water is sprinkled on each other by the dancers.

The dance is accompanied by the Chaupies and Chaumbaulas which sustain performance for hours. Women folk use twisted ropes, Kolars to mock-beat their counterparts. Men in a mood of frivolity wear women's costumes and exhibit their talent in female steps. The men folk not even a guest is spared. The dance is popular in Faridabad, Pulwal and Ballabhgarh. It is also performed in other areas.

Gangor-Puja Dance

This dance is performed in villages bordering on Rajasthan. It is ceremonial dance of woman in connection with puja ceremony of Iswar and Gangor (Lord Shiva and Pravati) dressed in colourful costumes and Jewellery, with brass jars on their head, the woman move in circle, the movements and the pattern of the dance changing according to the music. The smiles of the dancers are important element in the performance.

It is devotional dance to invoke the blessings of the gods for good harvest and is usually performed in the months of palghun and Chait. Sometimes the dance takes the form of a Kirtan, associated with the love of Lord Shiva and Parvati. The girls enter the circle one by one, dancing and singing devotional songs. The dance continues for hours.

Sapela Dance

Women often perform the Sapela dance in which one acts the role of the village belle while the other acts as the snake charmer.

9

Tribal Dances of Himachal Pradesh

Himachal is a land of dances. Its dance forms are varied and some are quite complicated. These dances are an inseparable part of tribal life which reflects the great perseverance and good humour of the human beings in the face of poverty and death. No festivity here is completed without dancing. The dance forms like Dulshol, Dharveshi, Drodi, Dev Naritya, Rakshas Nritya, Dangi, Lasa, Nati and Nagas are danced all over the state and provide a welcome break in the monotony of life. These last for hours and the beats and gestures keep changing from one stage to another.

The Mala (garland) Dance

The Kayang Mala dance is very popular in Himachal. In this, the dancers dressed in their traditional finery, weave their arms, together to form a sort of a criss-cross pattern so that, they appear like beads in an intricately woven garland. They drink chhang (a rice-brew) before the dance and that adds to the lusty beauty of the dance.

The Demon (Rakshasa) dance or Chhambha

These dances from the Kinnaur area are reminiscent of the pre-historic period. The Kinnaur folk are compared to playful deer. This dance form is performed with demon masks numbering three, five, seven or nine. It depicts the attack of the demons on the crops and their ritual chasing away by the forces of good.

'Chhambha' is similar to the Punjabi dance Bhangra. Dressed in their demon costumes and masks, the dancers look quite awesome. These dances are arranged in areas which have a dense population. During local festivals like Chaitol and Bishu, community dancing can be seen. In these men and women hold hands and dance. The leader is known as 'Ghure' and the rest follow in his footsteps. In some areas men and women dance separately.

The Dalshone and Cholamba dances

These dances belong to the Ropa valley and in these the patterns formed by the dancers look like coiled serpents. The Cholamba dance is performed when a tiger is killed. The skin of the dead animal is stuffed and a gold ornament is put in his nose. The carcass is then rotated and the people dance around it.

The Nagas Kayang is a dance which copies the movement of a snake. The Herki Kayang is faster in tempo and is danced to a romantic song. This dance is performed by young men and women. The Shuna Kayang dance is danced in most villages in the area and it combines both slow and fast movements. This depicts scenes from the life in the village as also the forest.

Jataru Kayang

This is a popular dance at festivals. In this dance songs connected with the festival are sung. As the musician play upon their instruments the leader of the dance, dances with a traditional Chamar in his hands The chamar becomes a great source of resentment and leads to fights among the dancers. The Ghure who is the leader of the dance has to deposit a small fee at the temple of the deity for using the chamar.

The Shan and Shabu dances

These are two popular dances of the Lahaul valley people and are danced at the Buddhist Gompas in the memory of the Buddha. Shan means a song of prayer for the Buddha. Dances danced to these songs are known as Shan dances. It is a tribal dance which is performed at the completion of the harvesting of crops. The instrument played in this are drums, shehnai and a stringed instrument like a violin.

A similar dance known as Shabbo is performed at festivals. It depicts the feelings and beliefs of the people in this area. These dances are linked to the local religious festivals.

Keekali and Bhangra

The Keekali (Kikli) dance is a dance of young girls and is danced playfully in twos. The girls hold hands crosswise and rotate fast on their toes, singing songs.

The Bhangra is a male dance which originated in Punjab and is popular in the Kangra, Himirpur and Una areas in a fairly wild form.

Rituals such as Chandroli, Jhumakada and Googa swang also give one a glimpse into the local dance forms.

The tribal dances of the trans-Himalayan region are different in content and music. The old tradition of both song and dance in these areas has been zealously guarded against any urban influence. The districts of Kinnaur, Lahaul and Spiti and Tehsils of Pangi and Bharmour of Chamba district constitute this zone. The inhabitants in these areas are known as Kinnauras, Lahaulas, Spitians, Pangwals and Gaddis. There are the Gujjars who are the wandering nomads. All these tribes have their own distinct traditions of folk-dances, songs, dresses and ornaments.

Besides the popular dances like Kayang, Bakayang and Banyangchu there are ritual dances performed by Lamas on certain religious ceremonies or festive occasions. One masked dance particularly features an important event in the history of Himalayan Buddhism when Lamas successfully carried out a plan of executing a cruel king Langdarma.

A special occasion for masked dances is the celebration of the birth of Padma Sambhava who is held in high esteem by the Buddhists of Himalayas since it was he who carried the message of Buddhism to Tibet.

In the sword dances of Kulu, men dancers dressed in the traditional tight white trousers and tunics with bright bordered shawls and black plumed caps decorated with blue primulas and yellow jasmine. The women dancers wrapped in woolen shawls wearing their colourful headgear (Dhatu) enter the arena.

Forming a circle and holding a handkerchief in the right hand men and women wave it as they move round and round in slight change and there are four steps taken with a pause in the fifth and three more steps with the flat of the foot. Then suddenly two or three dancers come into the centre of the circle and commence dancing with brandishing swords. The dance is accompanied by dholak, Ran Singha, Karnal and small Clarionets.

Nuala

Nuala is a folk dance of the Chamba valley. In this a garland is placed upon a pedestal as Shiva's garland and around it many dance dramas depicting scenes from the life of Lord Shiva are enacted. Women possessed of evil spirits are also brought to these gatherings and their antics also add to the general mystery and awesomeness of the spectacle along with the heady fragrance of the incense and the beating of the drums.

The chief devotee, Chela, of Shiva dances in a trance and answers questions that are put to him. He predicts dire changes and natural calamities which sends shivers in the crowds and people vow to offer special Puja if these are warded off by the gods.

Nati

Several forms of Nati dance are prevalent in the Kulu, Sirmaur, Mandi, Mahasu and Chamba areas. In Kulu this is known as Siraji Nati. It is like the Kathak dance and embraces a number of dances like Dheeli, Dekhi, Feh, Bakhali, Kahika, Dohari, Lahauli, Chambiyali, Banthada and Loodi. Rhythm is the main feature of this dance.

The instruments that accompany this dance range from Drums, Shehnai, Cymbals and Ranasinga (an instrument similar to a trombone). The Shehnai played by the Hesis is the life of the Nati dance. It not only provides a rhythm but also puts life into the entire performance.

The Nati is not a dance for professional dancers but is open for participation by all age groups. It is a slow-moving dance from Lasya variety and lasts through three or four days and nights. The costume for this comprises of Chola (top coat), Ghaghra (skirt), Gachi, Lachhi, a floral shawl and Boomani with silver chains, tight churidar pyjamas, socks and shoes.

The women wear heavy armlets and silver and gold ornaments known as Tunki and Chanki around their necks. The men and women hold an ornate fan in one hand and a colourful handkerchief in another and clap as they dance. Earlier the men and women danced separately but now they dance in unison.

The Jhoori, Gi, Swang Tegi and Rasa dances

The Jhoori, Thadair, Rasa, Gi, Nati, Swang Tegi, Draudi and Padua are popular dance forms of Sirmaur and the surrounding area. Jhoori is danced in the open. It is danced to questions and answers delivered in musical tones. Each line ends with Hoo Hoo sounds.

The Gi dance is performed to an intricate beat of three divisions. The singers stand in a circle and the dancers stand in the middle rotating with arms outstretched.

The Dhadair or Thadair is danced to the Rudra Tal. In this the dancers hold aloft weapon like bows, arrows, knives or sticks and yell too as they move towards their imaginary adversaries. This song repeat scenes from the local history.

In the Rasa dance, the dancers step back and forth and sit and leap up alternatively as they dance. This dance form is symbolic of the unity of the people.

Swang Tegi is a free dance which copies the gestures of animals. This is danced during the Diwali festival with the dancers wearing tiger masks carved out of wood. Dharvedi and Droondu are religious dances arranged during Jagaras or Shant. In these, scenes from the battlefields or temple and stupa shapes are presented. Dancing in circles and suddenly lying down on the ground and striking various poses are some of the chief features of these dances. These are danced with great fervour. These dances can be seen during the Dussera season in Kulu.

Khaydayat and Lamba dances

In these dance forms the dancers hold a sword in one hand and a scabbard in another and dance in a circle. The deft sword-play among the dancers is a delightful part of this dance and is more important than the musical or rhythmic aspect of dance. At the time the musicians quicken the tempo and the rest of the dancers cease to dance and stand quietly. The dance re-invokes memories of the feudal past.

The Lamba dance lays more stress on the movement of the feet. In this the dancers with first movement put the right foot forward and then the left and then the right again and in the fourth movement revert back to their original position. At the same time they clap their hands. It is a vigorous dance.

The Lahadi and Ghooghati dances

Lahadi is a popular dance of hill communities which is performed by women. In this, women form two teams which stand face to face. The singing is begun by women of the first team and the second team retreats as the singers bend at the waist, clap and move forward.

This is then repeated by the other team and the first team retreats to its original position. This lasts for a long time. This dance form employs no musical instruments and the dancers clap their hands.

In the Ghooghati dance the dancer stands in a line and the one behind puts his hand on the shoulders of the one in front of him. The first two or three dancers sing the song and the rest repeat the lines. This dance places a lot of importance on physical movement. As they sing the dancers move backwards and forward and bend sideways. This presents very interesting Choreographic composition.

The Dand Ras and Dangi Dances

The Dangi dances is a dance form of the Chamba area. It is performed at festivals, weddings and during Jatara by the Gaddi women, in lines and semi circular patterns. This is accompanied by the singing of the love ballads of Sunni and Bhukhu. The dancers join hands and move away by turns in this graceful dance.

The Danda Ras is danced to the best of complex rhythms like Dhamal and Lahauli on drums. The Lahauli beat goes slowly and in this the Gaddi dancers lower and raise their legs slowly as they dance in a circle uttering sounds like Jey Jey and Shee Shee. They wear their tradition costume of Chola-Dora and tight fitting Churidar pyjamas.

10

Tribal Dances of Jammu & Kashmir

The art products, specially the celebrated miniatures of Basohli (132 Km from Jammu, now a dilapidated township) have a pride of place in the great art museums of the world. The Amar Mahal Palace and the Dogra Art Gallery in Jammu, house collections of these exquisite paintings in the state.

An extraordinary terseness of the compositions, depicted with intense feeling and the utmost economy of line are the distinguishing features of the Basohli Qalam paintings. Another unique characteristic feature is their strong local flavour, typified by the brave romantic hero courting the frail but beautiful lady.

At the folk level, the typical art of the Jammu area can be seen on the walls of baulis or the constructions around a spring, usually in the vicinity of a temple.

As in different parts of India, the walls are usually ornamented with sculptures or engravings of gods and goddesses.

The naga provides a common motif for their ornamentations. Enduring specimens of Bauli art, noted for their excellence are to be found at Billavar, Sukrala, Sudh Mahadev and Udhampur. Wall paintings in the huts of villagers surprise the onlooker with the degree of artistry attained by the folk.

Dance

Dance, music and songs of the Jammu division also reflect the life of the folk, like the march of seasons, sowing and harvesting of crops, births, marriages and deaths.

Kudd is the popular dance of the upland dwellers. Usually performed at night after the sowing or other agricultural operations are over, Kudd starts with a slow rhythm, the dancers (wearing churidar and pyjamas or long robes falling to the knees) dance round and round a fire in an open space.

To the lively accompaniment of musicians playing on the flute, drum and narasinha, the tempo of the dance rises to a crescendo until the dancers, uttering loud cries are quite tired.

Another typical folk dance of the rural people of Jammu region, inhabiting the areas between the uplands and the plains is Phummian (the word meaning 'blooming', in Dogri). The gaily attired dancers open and close their fingers to symbolise the flowers in bloom.

Bhangra, the vigorous folk dance associated more with the Punjab, is quite popular among the people of the plains in the Jammu district. High-spirited revelry, the dancers leaping in the air, performing acrobatic feats, distinguish this virile dance, which has become a feature of marriage processions.

Particularly popular during the Lori festival in Jammu is the folk dance called Dandaras. An effigy made of bamboos and coloured paper, resembling a peacock, is carried by each group of dancers, who dance around it with gusto. Each one carries a short stick and dancer hits the sticks carried by the other group.

The skilled dancer is the one who can hit the sticks of others, himself gyrating in different postures

Music

As for Dogri-Pahari music, it has a long and rich tradition. Songs welcoming different seasons are accompanied with the virile Bhangra and other dances. The musicality of Dogras appears at its best in the singing of different forms of folk songs. The wind instruments used are nagaja (or galjoja), turturi, kail, narsinha and nafeeri. The stringed musical instruments are king, chakara and iktara. Among the drums, besides the dholki, nagar and duff are popular.

11

Tribal Dances of Karnatka

Folk Dance

Based on the content and purpose, folk dances of Karnataka are categorised as religious and secular.

Religious Dances

Most folk dances owe their existence to religion and are performed during fairs, festivals and other religious occasions celebrated by a local communities.

The dances like 'Nandi Dhwaja', 'Lingada-Berana', Gorava dance, Veeragase, Beesu Kamsale and Puravanthike are dedicated to the worship of Lord Shiva.

Bhagawanthike, Pata Kunitha and Bana Devara Kunitha are dances performed to worship Lord Vishnu.

Mariammana Kunitha, Urimarammana Kunitha, Puja, Karaga, Dollu, Soman Kunitha, Harige, Sedere, Bhoota Nrutya, Naga Nrutya, Vatte Kola, Kombat and Billat are being performed to worship all incarnations of 'Shakti', the deity of power.

Nandi Dhwaja

The dance performance in Nandi Dhwaja consist of an attractively decorated bamboo pole measuring about 20 to 25 feet long and 4 inch wide in circumference. Nandi Dhwaja is performed by skilled and experienced dancers. The performance begins with the erection of the Nandi pole which is initially thrust into a 'Navara'-the pouch worn by the performer. Balancing the pole at 90°, the dancer accomplishes rhythmic movements and intricate acrobats to the emotional tunes of the musical accompaniments. This dance is prevalent in all parts of the state except Kodagu.

Beesu Kamsale

The artistes of Beesu Kamsale are an expert singing community. But vigorous, rhythmic movements dominate the performance of Beesu Kamsale. Narration is regulated to the background.

Pata Kunitha

In Pata Kunitha, the major emphasis is more on the manipulation of pata (embellished bamboo pole, each measuring 10 to 15 feet high, carried by 10 to 15 artistes) than the narration. The dances Beesu Kamsale and Pata are widely popular in Mysore region.

Bana Devara Kunitha

In Bana Devara Kunitha, the folk artistes will be preoccupied with attaining perfect harmony to the clinking of bow bells rather than on oral communication of any religious content. The striking feature of this dance is archery. This form of dance is found in places like Hassan, Chitradurga and Chikkamagulur.

Puja Kunitha

In Puja Kunitha dance, the emphasis is more on the visual presentation than the oral narration. Here the spectacular exhibition of colourful bamboo structure is ably matched by the skilful body movements. It is prevalent in Bangalore and Mandya districts.

Karaga

Karaga is known for its rigidity with high ritualistic significance. It is popular in Mysore and Bangalore districts.

Sedere dance

In Sedere dance, the performance in an emotion charged atmosphere. Any communication through music gets drowned in the din of the thunderous sound of musical instruments amidst fast paced virile performance. Sedere is performed by scheduled castes and washer men in some parts of Bangalore and Hassan districts.

Gorava Mela

In Gorava mela which is extensively practiced in Mysore, Shimoga, Belgaum and Dharwad districts, the artistes display immense abilities of oral communication and perception. Goravas are singing tribe who narrates stories of deeper religious value.

Dollu

Dollu, a group dance which is widely practiced in Melkote in Mandya district offers a desirable atmosphere for the integration of new ideas in an unusual way, through interaction and exchange of information between the two groups of performers. Dollu, a semi circular dance, with a brilliant combination of sound and speed, performed by the Kurub community in North Karnataka, Shimoga and Chitradurga districts is worth noting.

The soul of Dollu Kunitha is the indigenous folk instrument called Dollu which when struck emits a thunderous sound. Mythological, historical and social themes are narrated by the chief narrator with the powerful musical accompaniment consisting of the Dollu, the cymbals and the flute providing appropriate musical setting to the narration. Messages on loan melas, small savings, adult education and population control programmes have been integrated into this folk dance.

Bhagavanthike

Bhagavanthike involves a competition of a witty dialogue between two groups of 10 to 12 artistes, who wearing spectacular costumes recreate the fanciful tradition of folk dance. Bhagavata, who is the chief narrator cum performer makes the folk dance of Bhagavanthike, a viable medium of non-formal communication.

There is also a jester. During the performance, the jester sings and dances along with other artistes sometimes following the traditional and sometimes setting up new precedents and serves as a change-agent. Attracting wider attention through his acrobatics, the jester skillfully adapts himself to the changing needs and demands of the audience eventually establishing a rapport with the audience with ease.

Mari Kunitha

The community dance, Mari Kunitha which is wide spread in Mysore and Mandya districts, display an insular flexibility in the presentation and narration. Originally belonging to the Shakti cult, these dances consist of performers standing either in rows or forming a big circle and dancing to the tune of 'Chakravaddya', an indigenous flat percussion instrument. The dance begins at a slow pace, gathers momentum, reaches a frenzied pitch as the tempo of the beat increases and continues till the rhythm fades away.

The songs are sung intermittently at each pause and hence could be heard by the audience clearly. In the dances like Kombat and Billat, which is similar to the Mari Kunitha, the artistes attired in customary 'Kodava' costume (consist of black robe, a silk waist belt and a 'Zari' bordered white turban) perform carrying deer-horns to the accompaniment of a drum and the dudi- a small drum.

Urimaramma

The folk dance of 'Urimaramma' is performed by a team of a husband and wife. The artistes are nomads, wandering from one place to another carrying an unusually designed mobile temple, eventually facilitating a simultaneous performance of dance and worshipping of the deity, right at the door of the people. The performer, acting like a messenger emphasises on a social problem and he tries to motivate the people to invoke the blessings of the deity so as to enable them to overcome an impending crisis.

Harige

Dances like Harige, Bhoota Nrutya, Naga Nrutya and Vatte Kola aim at appeasing the supernatural powers, lest the community is harmed. These dances are deep rooted particularly in the picturesque coastal region of South and North Karnataka. The dance serve as a traditional forum for community members to conduct a dialogue with the performer - the re-creator of ghost image, consequently paving way for a two way communication. The image of the ghost is most appealing.

Bhoota Nrutya

In the coastal region of South Kanara, the Bhoota Nrutya takes different forms, depending upon the type of the ghost it represents. Koratti, Koraga Taniya, Ali Bhoota, Punjurli, Kuppe Punjurli, Kalkuda, Kallurti, Shiradi Bhoota and many others represent a galaxy of ghosts worshipped in places like Puttur, Mangalore, Bantwal and Uppinangadi.

Naga Nrutya (snake dance)

The chief narrator of the Naga Nrutya (snake dance) is known as Vaidya or Patri. The dance is performed with religious fervour to appeal to the religious susceptibilities of the people.

Vatte Kola

Vatte Kola is another folk dance that comes under the umbrella of the Bhuta tradition. It is dedicated to ghost worship.

The presentation of Vatte Kola begins with the preparation of burning coal in an open field. The performers are required to walk over the burning charcoal pits. The performer of Vatte Kola is an excellent communicator who steals the show through his sincere worshipping of deity for the total welfare of the community.

Lingada Birana Kunitha

Lingada Birana Kunitha which is wide spread in the southern parts of the state and where the dancers perform splendidly, holding a sword in one hand and a shield bearing their religious emblem in the other to the tune of the devotional narration.

Puravanthike

Puravanthike is a highly expressive and credible narrative art which draws its strength from the heavy sprinkling of riddles in its content.

These riddles are folksy, woven around familiar things of daily life and also amuse people in the form of simple folk poetry and they serve as excellent channels of social education. In Puravanthike the costumes and ornaments are colourful. Dressed like warriors, the dancers present a skilful display of vigour with a sword in one hand and a trident in the other.

Secular Dances

If religious dances arouse religious sentiments of the people, the secular dances provide entertainment. Kolata, Chit mela, Marakalu Kunitha, Chennu Kunitha and Simha Nrutya are some of the important secular folk dances in the state.'

Chit mela

'Chit mela' which is performed by a group of ten artistes and is replete with colourful exhibition of eye-catching presentation is dominated by an unusual butterfly like display.

Chennu Kunitha

The folk art of Chennu Kunitha, the harvest dance found in Puttur, Coondapura and other villages of South Kanara give an insight into the cheapest mode of communication through entertainment.

Maragalu Kunitha

The folk dance of 'Maragalu Kunitha' consist of unique wooden legs which the artistes literally wear to gain unusual height. Wearing uniquely designed artificial legs the artiste easily captures the attention of the people through executing impressive but difficult feats.

Kolata

Kolata or stick dance is a kind of valour dance involving groups of people who indulge in bending, swaying and jumping activities to the tune of rhythmic clashing of sticks. With two sticks in hand, each dancer can strike in various patterns and rhythms. There is considerably more flexibility in the pattern of dancing so also singing. Members of Vokkaliga, Nayaka and Golla communities of Mysore, Mandya and Hassan districts and the Hallakki Gowda community of North Karnataka and the Kodavas of Coorg excel in Kolata. There is a rich spread of romantic and valour themes and references to contemporary, political and social issues in Kolata songs.

Alayi Hejje

'Alayi Hejje', a semi religious dance of the Muslim community of Karnataka, is a classic illustration of harmony between the two predominant communities of India, the Hindus and the Muslims. Jointly performed by both Muslims and Hindus, the presentation in Alayi Hejje consists of performers dancing around a fire pit. It appears like a rope dance with 20 to 25 dancers holding identical ropes which are hung from bamboo poles. The dancers form a circle and dance around the pole artistically winding and unwinding the ropes like plaits.

Alayi dance is an amalgamation of action and dexterous footwork, supported by appropriate devotional theme. Performed as part of 'Muharram' festival, Alayi Hejje provides a favourable forum for accomplishing the much needed communal amity in this much diversified society.

Serving as a symbol of communal harmony, the theme of Alayi Hejje can be explored for other purposes, than it presently expounds on the stage, besides its religious functions.

Simha Nrutya

The folk dance which is totally free from ritualistic and religious barriers is 'Simha Nrutya' (lion dance), the popular dance of the Honnavara taluk in the Uttara Kannada districts, usually performed by 'Yakshagana' artistes. The dance is in effect a charming imitation of a lion's movements. Hence the dancer wears a costume which closely resembles the lion. The costume is specially made of bark and yarn using natural dyes. The dancer wears a mask which is made up of cotton and is done to look like a lion's face.

Two silver pangs are inserted in the mouth to create a visual impression of fangs. With the perfect portrayal of a lion's behaviour, movements, mode of hunting and preying, Simha Nrutya is not only entertaining but educative also. Simha Nrutya, generally performed during the Yakshagana play is attracting attention and has been used in the propagation of messages like preservation of wild life, dangers of deforestation, dangers of poaching etc.

12

Tribal Dances of Kerala

Kathakali

Kathakali, is an efflorescent art form of Kerala. It has been described as a true representation of the artistic traditions of India and one of the most magnificent theatres of the imagination.

Kathakali is a highly stylised dance-drama which serves to present story themes derived from the Ramayana, the Mahabharata and other Hindu epics, myths and legends. The dance aspect consists of pure dance (nritya) as well as mime (abhinaya).

Kathakali was traditionally the preserve of men, but now women also perform the dance. The themes have also changed with times and the latest innovation is Shakespeare's King Lear.

What is most striking about Kathakali, is the emphasis given to aharya abhinaya, the use of costumes, ornaments and facial make-up. According to the qualities that they represent, the characters fall into five main types and the makeup illumines these types.

Kathakali makes strenuous demands on its exponents because it is the only dance form in which the entire body, both skeleton and muscles, down to even the smallest facial muscle are used to portray emotion.

The actor in kathakali never speaks expect with his hands. The text of the drama is sung for him and is the baseline for his interpretation. It is in histrionics or interpretive dancing that the Kathakali artist excels, the spectator's experience enhanced by the thrilling drum beats.

Mohiniyattam

Watch Video :Single Group

Origin

The Devadasi da[* File contains invalid data | Inline.JPG *]nce tradition which developed through the temple danseuses is an important form among the dance patterns of India. Mohiniyattam in Kerala took shape in the tradition of Devadasi dance which later grew and developed a classical status.

The special style of dancing developed by the Devadasis in Kerala was originally called 'Teviticci Attam'. Devadasis in Kerala were known by the general name 'Teviticci' which literally means - woman who serves at the feet of God

(Teviticci = Tevar + Ati + Acci; Tevar = God, Ati = feet; Acci = woman). Their dance was called 'Teviticci - Attam' (Attam = Dance). This later came to be known as Mohiniyattam by about 16th century AD. The word 'Mohini' literally means a maiden who excites desire or steals the heart of the on looker. It is a solo female dance (in a single costume) in which the striking features is the musical melody and rhythmical swaying of the dancer from side to side and the smooth and unbroken flow of the body movement. The dance is focused essentially on feminine moods and emotions.

There is the well known Puranic story of Lord Vishnu taking on the guise of a 'Mohini' to enthrall people both in connection with the churning of the milk-ocean and with the episode of the slaying of Bhasmasura. In the Bhasmasura story, 'Mohini' towards the end of her dance, persuaded the Asura to place his own finger on his head unwittingly to his own undoing. This episode seems to be picturesquely represented in the first item of the Mohiniyatam called

'Colkkettu' which begins with a pose of the dancer showing with her right hand, the murder of 'Suchimukha' with her first finger pointing to her own head. So Vaishnava devotees could have given the name of Mohiniyattam to this art form.

'Colkkettu' was also considered to be a dance pattern sacred to Lord Shiva. There is a sloka in praise of Siva towards the end of the text used for 'colkkettu' in Mohiniyattam.

Kerala has shared the general musical culture of peninsular India from the earliest times. South Indian music is generally known as 'Karnatic music' because of its common features. Each region of the south has its own culture. Kerala's music is known as Sopanam. Sangeetam (Music) appears to have acquired its name from the 'Sopanam' which means 'Sanctum Sanctorum' of the temple. Its essential features were born out of a happy blending of the Vedic, the folk and tribal music of the region.

The characteristic features of this music are, simple structure and peculiar forms of expression.

The structure of the Sopanam music is believed to reflect the experience of the devotee in ascending the heights of devotion. Sopanam music developed and became popular through the practice of singing invocatory songs in front of the 'Kalam' of Kali (floor drawing of Kali) and later on at the sanctum of the temple.

There are a few powerful schools connected with the temples like Pazhoor, Tiumandhamkunnu, Guruvayoor, Ramamangalam.

In these temples, this music had been hereditarily practiced by temple singers. Neralattu Rama Poduval of Tirumandhamkunnu bani, Janardhanan Nedungadi of Guruvayoor, Damodara Marar belonging to the Mudiyettu bant of Pazhoor are some of the most effective experts.

Sopanam music as it is practiced in different schools, maintains its rustic nuances with the feeling of devotion as its basic quality. From the temple sanctum this music has taken many diversions and grown as dance music in Ashtapadiyattam; the mould of which was later adopted by Krishnanattam, devotional music in Kalam pattu and dramatic music in Mudiyettu and Kathakali. In spite of its ramified developments, it failed to become pure concert music.

The system got the greatest rejuvenation when 'Geet Govindam' was introduced to Kerala in the local musical mould during the14th and 15th centuries A.D. It was certainly a revival of the pattu school of music which was preserved in the devotional tyanis (simple prayers of two line structure, sung at the sanctum of the temple along with different puja- ceremonial rites- at each time of the day).

The musician is inspired by the particular time, when the offering is made to the deity and he selects ragas which is most suited for that time. Such ragas are known as Samaya (time) ragas because time is the deciding factor in singing. The singing of tyanis takes its roots from the music of the earliest singers of the land as mentioned in the great text 'Chilappatikaram'.The value of Kerala music, its primitiveness, nativity and spontaneity can be assessed from its rudimentary usage preserved in the rustic musical and dance forms of a wide variety.

The region has maintained in its flourishing repertoire some of the rare melodies specially conceived for the purpose of embellishment of certain emotions. These melodies are 'Pati', Indisa', 'Puraniru', 'Kanakurinji'.

Certain other ragas like 'Sri kandi', 'Desakshi', 'Nalatha' and 'Samantamalahari' used in old devotional songs, can produce remarkably fascinating lilt and swing of a local character. The rhythm accompaniment to those songs with instruments like edakka, maddalam and chenda creates a parallel process of graceful rhythmic music bringing out the universality of sentiments with musical roots reaching into the past.

Literary Works

The genius of the people of Kerala for music could be seen from the days of 'Chilappatikaram'.

'Chilappatikaram' was originally conceived as a treatise of isai (music) which had two divisions; pan (full fledged raga) and tiran (its off shoot or Janya raga). There were innumerable varieties of tunes of ancient music created as a result of the combination of these pans and tirans. 'Chilappatikaram' (epic of Anklets), is a great integrative work. The author was a Chera Prince. The musical culture revealed in the work is very advanced. Vocal music had evolved to a high aesthetic sensitiveness and great technical sophistication. A variety of stringed instruments and percussion instruments are mentioned.

The rulers of the land managed to be adept in music. Kulasekhara of the fourteenth century and his brother Aditya Varma were great musicians. Aditya Varma has to his credit, the Vadasseri inscription of 1333 and also the fine message poem-' Unnineeli Sandesam'. Veera Kerala Varma, the great soldier- litterateur of the seventeenth century, translated Valmiki's 'Ramayana', composed a beautiful hymn of eight stanzas which has dexterously woven into its lyrical text the names of two dozen ragas.

Lyrical and musical masterpiece of the twelfth century, Jayadeva's 'Gita Govinda' drifted down to south and provided some stimulus to the rise of the dance-drama, Kathakali. In the eighteenth century, Ramapurath Warrier translated it into Malayalam. In many songs, he has scored the lyrics to the same ragas and talas as in the original, but in some cases he has attempted innovation.

The eighteenth century ruler of Travancore, Balarama Varma wrote an important treatise on music and dance entitled 'Balarama Bharatam'. He follows Bharata and the accent in his analysis is on dance, for which music is an indispensable accompaniment and embellishment. The treatment of music is detailed, especially valuable being descriptive classification of percussion, string and wind instruments.

Texts like the 'Sangita-Santram', the 'Sangita-Chudamani', the 'Sangita-Manjari', the 'Svarata-ladi-Lakshanam' etc belong to much earlier epochs. The publication and translation of these works will greatly enrich Indian musicology. There is a wealth of material in these texts. The 'Sangita-Chudamani' describes ninety ragas, several of them, have one hundred and one talas. Kunchan Nambiar created the dance recital form known as the Thullal. He composed many ragas like Mohana, Dvijavanti, Ananda Bhairavi and a variety of talas.

SWATI TIRUNAL

The greatest figure in Kerala's musical tradition who ranks one among the greatest personalities in the history of the Karnatic system of Indian music is Swati Tirunal. He wrote eight works, six of them in Sanskrit and two in Malayalam. They are mostly hymns and commentaries. His greatest contribution was in music. His musical compositions are supposed to number over five hundred.

Swati's ambition was to assimilate the best in all traditions and reutilize the native heritage. He invited to his court Kannayya, the disciple of Tyagaraja; the brothers Vadivelu, Meru Swami from Maharashtra; Lakshmana Das from Gwalior and Suleiman and Allauddin who were the exponents of the Hindustani music.

Swati has given songs in Sanskrit, Hindi, Telugu, Kannada and Malayalam. Besides 'Kritis', typical of the south, he has composed Dhrupads, Tappas and Khayals. Several of the compositions are in rare ragas like Saranganatta, Lalita Panchamam, Mohana Kalyani Dvijavanti and Gopika Vasantam. Some of these sacred songs are epitomes in a miniature, of the Ramayana and Mahabharata.

One of his brilliant achievement is Ragamala on the ten incarnations of Vishnu. Each stanza is a different raga. In many of his compositions he worked the name of the raga into the lyrical text in such a way that it becomes a word meaningfully fitted into narrative. He managed it in Ragamalas and in one instant, in a ragamala in Hindi.

The syllables pertaining to percussion instruments have been skillfully interwoven into the texture of some compositions like Nrityati in 'Sankarabharanam' and Sankara Sri in 'Hamsnandi'. The starting point in his kritis are varied. In Smarajanaka he has used atitagraha i.e. the song starts before the first beat of tala, slow and fast tempi are dexterously interwoven in kritis like Karunakara in Begada and Bhogindra in Kuntalavarali.

This virtuosity reached astonishing heights in the class of compositions known as Varnams. They are longer composition than kirtanas. Here Swati tried to weave the phemomes sa, ri, ga, ma which are the standard notation for the scale notes, into the lyrical text where they become accented and therefore conspicuous phonetic elements of words meaningfully used.

Swati was aiming at some pervasive spread of musical culture. He laid down what ragas should be sung or rendered in instrumental music every day at the Padmanabha temple,

Trivandrum. He composed kirtans for this daily service. He composed a Garland of nine gems, nine compositions. One for each day of Dussehra festival. He had cadjan leaf copies made of these compositions and distributed them to other centres in the state as well as outside it.

The stabilization of classical music in daily and seasonal ritual was a historical stop in the evolution of Kerala's musical tradition. Swati introduced the Harikatha or sacred recital from Maharashtra with the help of Meruswami. He invited Meruswami to his court especially for this purpose. The ruler himself wrote three extended compositions for such recitals. He has used Abhangas, Dinders and Chhands which are Marathi song moulds. Swathi used to compose songs in Malayalam and simple Sanskrit.

In every one of his kirtans, Swati preferred to use the name of the family deity, Sri Padmanabha. For him, the human soul becomes the maiden consumed by passionate longing for union with God's love. One of the kirtans expresses the emotions of a love lorn maid as the night deepens and each of its eight divisions goes by without her lover arriving. It is a ragamala of eight ragas.

The first raga is Sankarabharanam, the mode usually sung at nightfall and the last is Bhupala, the raga sung at the hour before dawn. The poetic tissue is rich in the familiar conceits of the Sanskrit tradition. Swati also brought in many Bharata Natya exponents from the neighbouring state, Tamil Nadu and contributed to the dance tradition in Kerala by composing fifty padams in Malayalam.

Folk Songs

There is a very rich folk song tradition in Kerala. Farmers, peasants; ploughing or harvesting and the boat men plying the oars on the palm-fringed back waters, forgot the tedium of toil by singing songs. Then the happiness of the harvest season, of the sacramental union of man and woman, of the advent of progeny also found expression in beautiful melodies.

Many classical composers also used this songs. Irayimmam Tampy, wrote a lyric for the melody of the traditional lullaby which is one of the most beautiful songs of this kind in Malayalam. Another lullaby melody was chosen by Cherrusseri in the fifteenth century to retell the Krishna story from the Bhagavatha in mellifluous verse in a Kavya of classical dimensions with forty-seven cantos. The boat song melody was used by Ramapurath Warrier in the eighteenth century for a fine narrative poem on the story of 'Kuchela' and by Kumaran Asan, for another narrative poem on the great compassion of the Buddha and the disciples who were inspired by him.

Mappila Patttukal (Mopla Songs)

The Muslim arts forms reflect the day to day life of the community through the songs which are generally known as Mappila Pattukal. These songs represent a long tradition of a happy blending of Arab and local elements of music. The language used in these songs represents a mixture of Arab, Persian, Urdu, Hindi, Tamil, Sanskrit and Kannada. It is believed that the rich literature of Mopla songs has a long history going back to 700 years.

The oldest known Mopla songs were mostly devotional dealing with the life of religious people. The earlier songs were extremely lyrical, highly imaginative and humanistic and earthly. These songs sung in rituals, household ceremonies like marriage and as a vocal accompaniment for dances. Love, heroism and devotion to God are the basic sentiments in these songs. The working people among the Muslim sing these songs to minimise the monotony and weariness of labour. There are songs which prop esoteric appeal. The songs of an erotic nature known as 'kess' are considered to be later addition.

Christian Songs

There were a lot of Christian songs in the pattu literature which were meant to propagate the Christian faith. One of the main songs deals with the life and deeds of St. Thomas. In the songs there is a touch of western music but the tunes are not all western. There is a very interesting blending of the folk tunes of Kerala. "Hitta Hinda Teyyakka Timrutai" forms the rhythmic basis for the lines. It is not the exact metre that is fixed by the meaningless syllables but only the pattern of rhythm. These songs were popular among the Christians converted from the lower castes of Hindu society whereas the aristocratic church songs, especially those sung in mass. It used to keep stronger ties with the Suriani music. But slowly these also came to be influenced by the folk tunes.

13

Tribal Dances of Madhya Pradesh

Gaur Dance

The most popular among the Madhya Pradesh dances, is the Gaur dance of the Sing Marias or Tallaguda Marias (bison-horn Marias) of South Bastar. This spectacular dance symbolizes the hunting spirit of the tribe. The word 'Gaur' means a ferocious bison. The invitation for a dance is given by sounding a bamboo trumpet or a horn. Wearing head-dresses frilled with stringed 'cowries' and plumes of peacock feathers fastened to them the men folk with flutes and drums make their way to the dancing ground. Women adorned with brass fillets and bead necklaces over their tattooed bodies soon join the assemblage.

They carry dancing sticks called Tirududi in their right hands and tap them to conform with the drum-beats. They dance in their own groups by the side of the male members. But they also take the liberty to cross and re-cross in between the groups of male dancers and drummers. Their jingling anklets correspond to the songs of their lips as they move. The men beat the drums, tossing the horns and feathers of their head-gears to the rising tempo that gives the dance a wilder touch.

The men with drums usually move in a circle and create a variety of dancing patterns when they are spirited. In the bison dance (Gaur) they attack one another and chase the female dancers. The Marias imitate a number of bison movements. Most of them perform like frisky bulls, hurling wisps of grass into air, charging and tossing horns.

Muria Dances

The Murias of North Bastar are trained in the Ghotul for all types of their community dances. Before any dance is commenced at a wedding or a festive occasion, the Murias first worship their drums. Very often they begin with an invocation to 'Lingo Pen', the phallic deity of the tribe and the founder of the Ghotul institution. To a Muria, Lingo Pen was the first musician who taught the art of drumming to the tribal boys.

The dancing site is chosen near the Ghotul compound. On marriage celebrations, the Muria boys and girls perform a dance called Har Endanna. The dance commences with a group of boys carrying ritualistic offerings and gifts and conducting the ridegroom to the ceremonial place.

In this light and happy dance, there are a variety of movements with the boy and the girl dancers and drummers participating to move in patterns with running steps and circles then changing directions, kneeling, bending and jumping. The movements of the drummers as they dance and manipulate their drums is fascinating.

Their Hulki is the loveliest of all the dances. The Karsana is performed for sheer fun and enjoyment. Both the dance-forms are quick and rich with many rhythmic nuances. In the Hulki, boys move in a ring while the girls tread way through them.

These forms are more favourite with the performing groups when they go to another village to attend wedding celebrations or else visit some fair. Their Pus Kolang expedition occurs in the month of February. During hot weather the boys and the girls meet in Chhat-Dadar expedition. Many of the dances associated to these visits are stick-dances.

Saila dance

Young boys of the plains of Chhattisgarh bring life to the post-harvest time by the Saila dance. Saila is a stick-dance and is popular among the people of Sarguja, Chhindwara and Baitul districts. But in these places, Saila is known by Danda Nach or Dandar Pate. The Saila often comes out with many variations and much buffoonery.

Sometimes the dancers form a circle, each standing on one leg and supporting himself by holding on to the man in front. Then they all hop together round and round. Sometimes they pair off, or go round in a single or double line, occasionally, climbing on each other's back. The climax of a day's Saila, is the great Snake Dance. The Saila songs, of which the refrain is the monotonous Nanare nana are usually of a progressive character leading to a highly vulgar conclusion.

Saila comprises over half a dozen varieties. Some of them are named as the Baithiki Saila, the Artari Saila, the Thadi Saila, the Chamka Kunda Saila, the Chakramar Saila (lizard's dance) and the Shikari Saila. Each variation has a certain theme and distinctive feature of its own. Saila's simple form is the Dasera dance which is always performed by the Baigas before Diwali. Some of the post-harvest dances reach the climax towards the festivities of Diwali.

The Diwali dances of the Ahirs and Rawats of Bilaspur and Raipur districts of the state have enough of vital appeal. Wearing tight-fitting shirts, studded with ghungrus or tiny bells and armlets of ghungurs, the Ahir dancers vigorously perform the Danda dance.

Karma dance

Among the Gonds and the Baigas of Chhattisgarh and the Oraons of the north-west fringes of Madhya Pradesh, the Karma dance is very common. This form is associated with the fertility cult and essentially related to the Karma festival that falls in the month of August. The Karma dance symbolizes the bringing of green branches of the forest in the spring. Sometimes a tree is actually set up in the village and people dance round it. The dance is filled with breath of trees. The men leap forward to a rapid roll of drums. Bending low to the ground the women dance, their feet moving in perfect rhythm to and fro, until the group of singers advances towards them.

The Majhwars of Sarguja district dance the Karma towards the beginning and the end of the rainy season. The Gonds and the Baigas of Mandla and Bilaspur districts dance it at any time they wish. The Baigas, the Jhumies, the Kanwars and the Gonds of Baghelkhand area perform this dance to the accompaniment of the Thumki, the Payri, the Chhalla and the Jhumki instruments. The Sirki, the Ghatwar, the Jhumar, the Ektaria, the Pendehar, the Dohoari, the Tegwani and the Lahaki are some of the sub-varieties of the Karma dance.

There are other variants of the Karma. The songs associated with these variants differ with each pattern. The Thadi, the Lahaki, the Khalha, the Jhumar and the Jharpat are the variations of Baiga Adivasis dance. The Karma seems to have been the oldest dance form of the Adivasis of Madhya Pradesh. It is the only dance which is common to the many ethnic groups of India.

Kaksar Dance

The dance of the Hill Marias of the Abujhmar mountains is quite different. In one of their dance-forms they carry dummy horses on their shoulders and move slowly into a wide circle.

Kaksar is a festival dance, performed by the Abhujmaria of Bastar. Prior to the rains, the Maria cultivators in every village worship the deity for reaping a rich harvest. To invoke the blessing of the deity, Kaksar, a group dance, in which young boys and girls take part, is performed. Boys put on a peculiar costume of a long white robe while girls are clad in all their finery.

The dance presents to both girls and boys, a unique opportunity to choose their life partners, and marriage is enthusiastically celebrated afterwards. There is a rhythm and melody in this dance. The melodious music, the tinkling of the bells combine to create an atmosphere of spell and enchantment.

Chaitra festival dance

The Chaitra festival dance is another famous dance of the Gonds of Bastar district; it is performed after the harvest to thank goddess Annapurna for the harvest already gathered and to seek her blessings for the next crop. Men and women dance in a circle, in semi-circles or in rows; all dancers hold each other's waist.

A peacock feather on the head is a distinctive mark and the dancers wear colourful costumes, adorning themselves with garlands of shells and pearls. As the dancers go round in rhythmic movements, their feet beat to the music of the Shehnai, Nagada, Timki, Tapri, Dholak and Maduri. Sometimes, the Singha and Kohuk; wind instruments are also played.

The Rina is the women's dance. It is called Tapadi among the Baigas. The Gond women of Mandla district start the Rina just after the festival of Diwali.

Sua or Sugga dance

The Sua or Sugga dance of the women of Chhattisgarh and the Mikal Hills is significant for its elegance and grace. The word 'Sua' means a parrot. The women take recourse to this dance a month in advance of the festival of Diwali. While dancing, the women lift their feet in imagination of a parrot-walk, then bend and jerk their heads in bird-like fashion to the clapping of hands. Groups of girls often go on long trips to the adjoining villages to display their excellence in this dance. Similarly they receive groups of girls visiting their own village. They prepare a wooden Sugga (a parrot) and place it on an earthen pot covered with paddy shoots. One of the girls carries the pot on her head and stands as a revolving figure in the middle of the group to face the dancing row when the opposite row of the girls alternatively stops. In this dance no instrument is used with the exception of a wooden clapper named Thiski is played to provide rhythm, where the Gonds and the Baigas predominate.

The folk-dances of the hilly tracts of the Vindhyas are more indigenous and recreational. Not a single ceremonial occasion passes in any community without dance and music. The Bhils who inhabit the Vindhya ranges and the banks of the Narmada are traditionally prone to their Bhagoriah and Gavar dances. Their instruments are an ordinary Mandal (big drum) and a Thali (brass plate). Hundreds of men and women join and move in a circle with wild shouts and lusty songs to the noisy abandon of the beat of drums.

The Bhagoriah is typical of ecstasy and vibrating spectacle. Men waving bows and arrows synchronize their movements and stamping of feet with verve. During the Holi festival in Phalguna (Feburary) the Bhils and the Garasias perform a dance called the Ger. The women of both these tribes also dance the Loor. They form a circle and then holding their hands, they dance the Loor with forward and backward movements. In the Pali dance, the women form two rows. The Duipali, the Pachmundya Pali and the Ondi-Chiti Pali are the other forms of the Pali dance.

Folk-dances of nomadic tribes

Some of the indigenous folk-dances of Madhya Pradesh are by nomadic tribes like the Banjara and the Kanjar of Bhopal commissionary. In this area, one comes across a dance form known as Lehangi. In the middle of the rainy season when nature comes to bloom the Lehangi is danced by young men over the beat of sticks which they hold in their hands. The Kanjars are professional acrobats. They dance with full poise and acrobatic tricks.

On the Rakhi festival, the Banjaras of Nimad dance the Lehangi. When the festival of Dussehra approaches they start dancing Garbi and Dandia. Banjara dancers have a remarkable similarity in their mode. The men accompany the women either with songs or instruments. The Banjara women are heavily decked with silver jewellery and wrapped in colourful clothes of contrasting embroidery and tiny inset of scintillating mirrors. In the Lota dance, with all the ornaments and heavy clothes, they balance big-size metal pots on their heads as they swing in a liner or a circular formation.

Matki dance

The tableland of Malwa has comparatively very few dances. On wedding occasions, the countryside women of this part perform the 'Matki' dance with an earthen pot balanced on the head, the Matki is mostly danced solo. Sometimes just for merriment a couple of women join the main dancer who usually dances with a veil on her face. The two other variations of the Matki are the Aada and Khada Nach.

Phulpati Dance

The Phulpati is another dance, exclusively for unmarried girls. It is a dance of the semi-rural womenfolk. The agriculturist class of Malwa is not very much inclined to any dance by nature. During the Holi festival the revelers cannot restrain themselves from coming out with some sort of dance movements to the uneven manipulation of drums.

Grida Dance

When rabi crops sway in the fields in full bloom, the parties from different villages join together and perform the Grida dance. It continues from morning till evening. The host village returns the visit next year by going to the village of their guests of the preceding year. The dance has three distinct phases:

(1) Sela - The feet movements are slow and comparatively rigid.

(2) Selalarki - The feet movements become brisker and faster.

(3) Selabhadoni - With the acceleration of the tempo, every limb of the body begins to sway in mood of exaltation.

The Attire

The men wear white muslin turbans or occasionally silk ones. The turban is adorned with a coronet of peacock feather stems. Down to the waist they wear a close white Saluka or blouse, below a dhoti of small width coming down to the knees, the end of which hangs loosely behind. On their necks hang necklaces of silver or gold coins or corals. Their hands are adorned with silver bangles and their feet with heavy brass or iron, boat-shaped ornaments which tinkle to the timing of the rhythm. In their right hand they hold a staff, in their left a white kerchief or peacock feathers.

The costumes of the musicians are different from those of the dancers. They put on a shirt or a jacket and coloured turbans; they do not use cowries.

The women wear a coloured dhoti, wound close round the body down to the knees, one end of which goes up across their breasts to their backs. The knot of their hair is adorned with a coronet of palm or other leaves behind which hangs a net of corals.

From their necks also hangs a chain of coins or corals. Besides the necklaces of coins or corals they wear silver hansali also. In their ears, they wear heavy silver ear-rings from which hang small slender silver chains. Besides, they wear bahunta (armlets) on their arms, silver bangles on their wrists and perry or todar round their ankles. While dancing, in their right hand they hold thiski (a clapper) and in their left a coloured kerchief.

14

Tribal Dances of Maharashtra

Maharashtra has a lively tradition of song, dance, music and theatre. Vasudev, a dance form, is performed by people believed to be incarnation of Lord Krishna. Bedecked in the distinctive headgear of peacock feathers, performers sing Vasudev geets and with nimble, delicate dance steps, whirl around presenting anecdotes from Lord Krishna's life in exchange for alms. Soothing, melodious notes float through the villages, particularly near Jalgaon and Dhule.

On auspicious occasions like the birth of a child, dancers might hold night- long performances called gondhals. Elsewhere, rustic actors could be narrating lively stories through the bharud, an enactment of the written musical compositions of poet- saints, and singers could be crooning powadas, inspiring ballads.

The lavni performed by women, is sometimes called the queen of Marathi folk music and dance. It is incorporated in slapstik tamasha, and is perhaps one of the most popular folk forms. Marathi theatre itself has evolved over the years, and is now a mature form of communication which challenges norms and often embraces rebellious themes.

Crafts

Maharashtrian jewelers are busy at work, creating ornaments for villagers, dancers, business women and brides. Remains of old intricately carved woodwork can still be seen in palaces of yesterday, and in tiny shops in the bylanes of Nashik metal workers style utensils and vessels following age-old traditions. Paithan, which was once an important seat of learning, is famous for its beautiful silk saris which sport intricate gold borders. In Aurangabad, families weaves silk-like himru shawls and make silver bidri ware.

Chawk, the sacred pictograph of the Warlis was traditionally painted by women during wedding ceremonies. The technique involves the use of rice paste and straw which is smeared on the mud walls of their simple dwellings. The central figure here is of Palghat, the goddess of trees and plants, who symbolises creative energy. Today, young men have taken to painting their own experiences, using the typically decorative Warli motifs on paper.

15

Tribal Dances of Manipur

DANCE

Lai - Haraoba

The Manipuris believe that this dance represents the concept of the beginning of the world. There is a legend that in the beginning there was only Guru Sidaba, the highest Lord, existing in the dark vacuum. Once the brilliant hues of the rainbow shot into this dark space, the beams of lights motivated the Guru to witness the world with flora and fauna.

He sent Atiya Guru Sidaba along with a creature to create the world. This creature spun a web-like frame work on which the human inhabitation was to be initiated. Atiya Guru desired to solidify the framework.

He went again to Guru Sidaba. The Guru offered him some dirt from his navel and he also created nine men from right side and seven women from his left side to assist Atiya Guru. The dirt was to be applied to the framework to solidify it. The Atiya Guru along with the team of men and women sat down to work.

Their attempt was foiled twice by one Harba. Guru Sidaba then sent the goddess of lightning to assist Atiya Guru. With the graceful beauty and charm the goddess could entice Harba away. The framework was then solidified and declared fit for human habitation. On its completion the occasion was celebrated as Lai-Haraoba. Twelve main sequences which part by part depict each process in the creation.

Nongdai Jagoi : The dance of commencing the split in the sky, the splitting of the rainbow in the sky by the Guru Sidaba. The hands are moved skywards in trying to bring the two parts together. In Leitai Dance, The waist is moved in circular movements depicting the spreading of earth dirt on the web-like framework. When the earth was completed and divided into different divisions, the dance started by moving hands from side to side.

Leitai Dance depicts the formation of the trace with the dirt from the Guru's navel. The dance steps are done on tiptoes. Lai-Haraoba is performed in worship of gods like Pakhangba, Thangjing etc. It has got three main forms. The Kanglei Lai-Haraoba is celebrated at the palace. The Moirang Lai-Haraoba is celebrated in the honour of Lord Thangjing and the Chakpa Lai-Haraoba which is basically observed by Loi people.

Lai Haraoba takes place in Manipuri month of Kalen (April/May). It continues for a week. There are certain days of the month which are considered propitious and the festival is celebrated on these dates like 1, 2, 3, 5 and 8. The deities are represented by a pair of bamboo tubes, wooden or brass mark with cloths placed below and above, pieces of wood or iron or a coin etc.

The dance is divided into seven sections. First section is the Lai Ikouba. This consists in calling the Lai out of water. The Maibi sits before water from which Lai is called up, chanting incantations and ringing a hand-bell. It is called Laimang Phamba (sitting before the Lai). Second is the Laibou Jagoi which is a dance with antiphonal singing, representing the life cycle of Lai. Third is the Panthaibi Jagoi which is a dance depicting the romantic tale of Nangpok Ningthou and Panthoibi. The episode is always danced in Naga costumes. Some expressions of jhuming cultivation are also expressed during this dance. It may be of Tangkhul origin. Fourth is the Lairen Mathek.

It is a communal dance in which the circular pattern representing the python is danced. It is limited to Kamglei Haraoba and is related to the python manifestation of Pakhangba. Basically it is related to the royal clan, the Ningthouja. Fifth is the Ougri Hangel. It is also a communal dance designed to bring wealth and prosperity. Sixth is the Thoubal Chongba. It is called the dancing by moon light in circle. It has seasonal importance. In the month of March/

April after 'Yaosang' (Holi), this dance is performed in the Mandapas of Temples or in the open air.

Boys, girls and grown up people take part in its performance. The Thoubal Chongba offers a chance to express the element of excitement and activities in dance form. In villages and towns the organisers arrange a beautiful illumination by fitting the tube lights on bamboo posts around a sufficient area which is centrally located public places. In the moon-lit night the dances go on till late at night. Boys and girls dance together in a group forming a long chain. The dancers may join and leave at different intervals at their own convenience. Seventh is the Nongkarel at the end of the festival. The Lai-Haraoba is the combination of religious recitations, traditional music and dance, traditional social values and ancient cultural aspects.

Tribal Dance

The tribal dances are part and parcel of the Manipuri dances. It provides an evolutionary trend of dance styles. The tribal dances are the most natural. The dance was started by copying the nature. They perform war dances. they also developed some sacred dances from their experience of spirits and superstitions. Such dances are performed to please the spirits. The tribal dances of Manipuri Nagas are very famous.

The men wear a coloured loin cloth round the hip, scarf crossed at chest hanging down on each, the front and back, its cloth is with multi coloured bands, the leggings white or coloured, in hand the Dao or spear is carried. Unmarried girls generally take part in the dance. They wear skirt by wrapping around their body the tinsel ornaments in circles round the hair-knot on the head. There are several kinds of dances.

In Hansengav the boys and girls form a circle. The steps are taken with music and alternately changed. The movement is slow in the beginning and also the music goes slow but gradually it is allowed to increase to the climax.

The dance ends when the male dancers come closer in the circle and hold their Daos by exposing them in the air.

In Toonaga Lomna also girls and boys forms a circle. They dance but the circle as a whole moves slowly at the centre two couples face each other. The girls exchange while turning round and round. The steps are taken with the tune and changed alternately.

Boys and girls forms two parallel rows in the dance Heng Naga Toona. The hands are clasped by the two opposing each other. These are swung up and down with music, the rows move with taking steps side to side alternately. Towards the end two or four girls dance in the centre to finish the dance.

In Tinkoom Gueina Tonagga Lamay dance girls and boys form a circle which is stationary and two girls dance in the centre. They show fantastic movements of their hands with the music.

The dance Chan Lam is performed only by the men forming a circle and they move, the step is taken forward then backward to its position and then again forward. While they move everyone shouts ho! ho! ho!. The dancers divide and then form a party dance is irregular pacing with quick music and at last the dance is finished with howls. The Kukis also perform these four types of dances. The Kukis were inferior tot he Nagas in dances, though superior in singing.

The Lushais of Churachandpur perform a beautiful dance called Bamboo dance.It is performed by girls. The costume of the dancer is colourful. The skirt is of a colourful combination of horizontal and vertical stripes. The block carry geometric designs of varied colours. The skirt is tied at the waist and goes down to cover the thighs and leg up tot he feet. The upper body is covered with blouse. The head-dress is unique. A ribbon of bamboo strip encircles round the head with plumes adjusted around.

At the back of the head the ribbon carries a horizontal rod like a bob kin with strings hanging down. The dancers perform the dance by lightly jumping over the bamboo sticks. The bamboo sticks are placed horizontally in parallel spacing over the vertically placed bamboo sticks to form criss-cross. Two women, each sitting on one side, slide the horizontal bamboo sticks over the vertically placed bamboo sticks on the ground, with the rhythm of the music. The striking of the sticks also produces the music. The dancers adjust rhythmic helps of their feet according to the music.

16

Tribal Dances of Meghalaya

Dance

Dances are held at an open ground or premises of felling sad and public places. There are two traditional dances of the Khasis.

1) Shad Sukmynsiem or Weiking dance

2) Shad Nongkrem or Pomblang Nongkrem

The Shad Sukmynsiem (Dance of the Blissful Heart) is popularly known as Shad Weiking. It is so called after the name of the ground where the dance used to be held every year. A thanksgiving festival, Shad Suk Mynesiem is a symbolic offering of salutations to God, homage to their ancestors and proclamation of unity of the Khasi people. There is no fixed date for this dance.

It used to be held during the month of April of each year. This is the most popular dance among the Khasis. It is organised by the Seng Khasi (Khasi Religion). The dances last for three days. Only unmarried men and women are allowed to take part in the dance. Youngsters and damsels from different part of Khasi hills participate in the dance. The Shad Sukmynsiem welcomes the whole of the Khasi community to take part in the dance.

There was no bar for any one to take part in the dance since it is the traditional dance of the Khasis. Christians or Hindus as long as they belong to Khasi community could take part in this dance.

Young lads brilliantly clad in colourful silk dhotis, coat and a plumed turban and adorning glittering ornaments look like Rajput Princes.

They dance around with a sword or spear in one hand and a plume in the other. Pretty maidens in magnificent many-splendoured silk-robes and elaborately decked in priceless intricately designed ornaments of gold and silver and wearing a silver crown emerge before use as apsaras from the world beyond.

These 'angels' move in an inner circle in two's and three's in tiny steps while the lads form a protective ring around them and flashing their weapons. The embroidery on the girl's apparel and the workmanship of their ornaments, many of them handed down for generations as heirlooms, can made even an aristocratic millionaire envious. It is difficult to see how the European missionaries could so heartlessly condemn these fine expressions of blissful hearts as 'barbaric'.

The dancers dance rhythmatically making regular movements and keeping time with the beat of thc drum and pipe (Tanguari). Damsels (unmarried) dressed colourfully in their very originality and making tiny steps in the centre while men folks with swords and sometimes with shields in their hands encircling them.

Another folk dance of the Khasis, Shad Nongkrem is associated with Ka Pomblang Nongkrem. Like all other ceremonies of the Meghalayans, it is performed to propitiate the all powerful Goddess Ka Blei Synshar for a rich bounteous harvest and prosperity of the people (subject). There is no fixed date for this festival. It is generally celebrated in November of every year.

The Syiem of Khyrim accompanied by the high priest performs the Pomblang ceremony. He offers oblation to a Lei Shyllong; the god of Shyllong peak by sacrificing a cock. Goats are killed during the ceremony.

The Nongkrem dance is associated with the Pomblang Nongkrem. When the ceremony has been performed by the Syiem and the high priest, the Nongkrem dance starts. At drawn-break on that day a maiden dance is held in which virgins from the Syiem house take part and the Syiem Sad shaded by an umbrella, dance with great solemnity.

This is called an opening dance or royal dance which is generally done by the Syiem before the dance starts. When the royal dance is finished, youngsters and damsels of the Khyrim Syiemship enters the field and the dance of

U Khun U Raiot (subjects) of the Hima Khyrim (Khyrim Syiemship) starts. The dance lasts for three days, the last day or the third day is the biggest of all. Unmarried males and females from four corners of the Khyaim Syiemship take part in the dance.

Another dance among the Khasis is Doregata in which the women try to knock off the turbans of their male partners, using their heads. Another dance that the performer dangles a pomelo or any other fruit on a cord tied to his waist and then whirls it round and round after the initial impetus with a barely perceptible movement of his hips. Some experts can control two separate pomelos in this way.

The Garos have traditional dance called Do Dru-su'a in which two women dance like doves pecking each other.

For entertainment, the Pnars have their Laho dance, in which members of both sex participate in their festival finery. Usually two young men on either side of a girl, linking arms together dance in steps. While in place of pipe and drum there is a 'Cheer leader', usually a man with the gift of impromptu recitation who recite disrespectfully humorous lines for the enjoyment of the audience.

17

Tribal Dances of Mizoram

The dances of the Lushais, pawis and Lakhers are mostly common. Most popular of the Mizo dances now is the cheraw or the bamboo dance. Six girls wearing colourful, ceremonial dresses and flower crowns as head gears squat on the ground holding bamboo poles which are rhythmically shifted and struck against one another. Six other girls dance, moving between the shifting bamboos. The dance has a fast rythm and symbolises the pulsating youth. Bamboo dance, exactly in this forms, is found in some south-east Asian countries, notably in the phillipines.

Khal Lam is another popular dance of Mizos in which a group of boys wearing specially made shawls dance to the beat of drums and gongs. The dancers wear one type of striped loin cloth (puan) and a uniform striped shawl (puandum). While one beats a gong, the dancers in a row more gradually forward, with small forward-backward steps, keeping with the time. The arms would be flayed, along with the steps.

On occasions of Chapchar Kut festival the boys and girls would dance chaithe whole night. The boys would sit with their backs to the wall. Each boy would have a girl sitting in front of him, in between his knees, with her back towards him. Individual dancers would perform in the clearing in the middle, all the others joining in the music.

The young folk would perform another type of dance in the open courtyard. They would make a circle with a girl in between two boys with their arms over the shoulders of the girls. In the midst of the circle, one would beat a drum or gong and all in the circle would move forward and backward and would also progress slowly along the circle. The person in the middle would chant a song and the refrain would be taken up by all. All the time the dancers would get rounds of Zu and the dance would last as long as the supply of Zu could be kept up.

Another popular dance is Sawlakin. This was originally a Lakher dance, but now it has been adopted by all the Mizas. Sawlakia means spirit of the slain. The dance was led by the warrior who had hunted a big game or killed a man. He would wear his best clothes and a plume of red feather. He would wield a gun or dao and a shield.

He would be followed by other dancers in a row, who would also carry weapons, or cymbals or gongs. Some boys would stand in a group beating drums or blowing bugles. The dancers would move forward and slowly go round the head. While dancing weapons and shields would be wielded keeping time with drum or gong beats. All the time dancers would be plied with Zu by the women. This dance is a popular dance now. The modifications now are that there is no head in the circle and no Zu.

The Chhilam was the dance performed in beer parties. But this dance still continues in a modified form, particularly in gatherings at homes. This is danced by elderly people and mostly by men, but sometimes women also join in. The men and women sit in a circle, beating the drum, and sing anecdotes and each takes a turn to dance in the centre of the circle.

Mizo traditional songs and dances were the common amusements of the people. A Zu party would always be an occasion for songs and dances. The songs were slow and generally sounded mournful. Songs would be accompanied by beat of drums or gongs.

The theme would mostly be narration of some events or praise of some hero or former villages, description of some hunt or simply of love. In a gathering of Zu party or on the occasion of marriage or after a successful hunt, one would start the music by reciting a verse and it would be followed by singing of the verse by all others and this would continue in the same sequence for a long time sometimes even throughout the night.

The young Mizos have, in the recent past, taken up western music and dances with great aplomb. In all the villages, groups of young men and women gather in the evening and sing and dance, sometimes the whole night.

The only musical instrument used is the Spanish guitar, called ting tang by the Mizo. The young Mizos, both boys and girls, have a very lilting musical voice and they have a natural flair for music.

A very recent development is pop music with a composite band which is popular in towns and big villages.

MUSICAL INSTRUMENTS

The traditional musical instruments of the Mizos had been mostly the drum, gong and flute. The drum are made from hollowed out tree trunks two sides of which are covered by fine hides. It is about a foot in diameter and two feet in length. The drums is used in all feasts and festivals and it keeps beat in songs and dances. The gongs are made of brass and come in various sizes.

These have always been imported from Burma and are rather costly. Gongs are sometimes played in a combination of three: each gong having a separate note the three gongs would together produce a tune. Another instrument used was made of gourds in which hollow reeds were inserted. The player would blow through one reed and would produce a tune by opening and closing holes in the other reeds. Flute was made from bamboo pieces. Now-a-days however, only the drum and gong are used.

18

Tribal Dances of Nagaland

MUSIC AND DANCE

Music is an essential accompaniment to any Genna or festival. The themes have a wide range of variety. They may glorify a tradition, extol a specific act of heroism, narrate an important event of the recent past or relate to a love story. A common musical instrument played by the Nagas is Petu. It is a string instrument. The Angamis and Chakhesangs are particularly fond of it and it is used to give the desired accompaniment to one's voice. Another popular string instrument is Theku. Of the wind instrument, the flute is quite common.

In earlier days, the instrument was kept in the Morung only, but now the restriction is not observed. In some tribes, only boys are allowed to play the flute, the girls are debarred lest they seduce the young boys. The trumpet is mostly used by the herds men to scare away wild animals from the cattle. Among the present-day youth, the guitar is very popular. Born and brought up in a Christian atmosphere, the young boys and girls are naturally attracted to western music and instrument.

Dance

Dancing is natural to the Naga tribes. It is full of vigour and vitality. Strangely it is the monopoly of men, except in Zeliang tribe where women join with their men folk in dancing. There is nothing like individual performance.

Naga dancing is always in a group. It is difficult to generalize, but roughly it could be said that the artists first slowly enter the arena or stage, make a circle or any other geometrical formation and gradually work up tempo with the stamping of feet, interspersed with clapping and chanting of some formula. The spear, dao or the shield are swung to the rhythm of the dance. After the climax is reached, the tempo is brought down again and there is a satisfying finale. The beauty of the dances is heightened by the colourful costumes. The zeliang dance is particularly artistic.

The Zemis of North Cachar hills are very fond of dances. There are a number of dances and each with a different name. They are named after the manner in which hands and feet are executed to resemble the movements of a bird or an insect or an animal. For example, Nruirolians known as 'cock dance' is the dance which resembles the trait of a cock, Gethinglim or 'cricket dance' is a dance in which hands are moved to and fro.

Some what resembling the movement of the insect Temangnetin or the 'fly dance'; Hetateulee or the 'bear dance', which was usually done by men when defeating enemies. All these dances are performed with the accompaniment of songs and music. Drums and cymbals are beaten at regular intervals while the singers array themselves on one side or form a circle so as to allow space for the dancers in the centre. Songs which are generally and commonly sung by both young and old alike may be classified as follows.

Songs

1. Heliamleu or dancing songs - They are composed and sung by young and old alike and are usually romantic.
2. Hereileu or war songs - composed by old people about the pride of their life, their bygone days, usually sung in memory of the victory or defeat in war.
3. Neuleu or legendry songs - composed by old men to commemorate any significant event of the old days or that of a person who had done something notable during his life time.
4. Hekialeu or songs about self - These songs are composed by old men of their eventful career while they were young and strong.
5. Hekialeu or a duet - composed by both young and old is sung by young boys and girls together.

19

Tribal Dances of Orissa

DANCE

'Odissi', the traditional dance of Orissa, has been accepted as an important classical form of Indian dance for its exquisite beauty and charm. Among the folk dances of Orissa, 'chhau' has earned world-wide reputation.

Chhau Dance

The basic postures and stance of this dance resemble the postures of a combatant in a traditional fight. In its rudimentary form it is generally referred to as Phari Khanda Khela (the game of sword and shield) or Rookmar Nacha (the dance of offence and defence). Thematically, Chhau draws substantially from the Ramayana and the Mahabharata.

Themes drawn from the Krishna legend are also many. Most of the themes are puranic episodes like the fight of 'Abhimanyu' with the 'Sapta Rathis', the killing of 'Mahishasura', 'Shiva Tandav', 'Kirat Arjuna', 'Jambeb', 'Garuda Bahana', etc. The Krishna themes like 'Bastraharan', 'Kalanka Bhanjan', 'Nisitha Milan', 'Banshi Chori' and 'Tamudia Krishna' are predominantly erotic in mood and draw heavily on the local folk tradition. There are also significant tribal themes like 'Sabara Toka', 'Kala Chakra', 'Sabara Sabaruni'.

The themes of Chhau are thus largely drawn from the puranic and combine elements of tremendous kinetic fury and very fast footwork with mellowed elegance and lyricism which is at times indistinguishable from visual poetry.

Naga Dance

The dancer has a heroic feature and wears a special dress. He dances with a heavy load of weapons to the sound of the battle drums. He has ten main requirements, Viz.

(1) A shield of the hide of the rhinoceros,

(2) a sword,

(3) a Kukri,

(4) a gun,

(5) a horn used as a whistle,

(6) an iron shield,

(7) a toilet box,

(8) bow and arrows,

(9) tiger skin, and

(10) a bell.

His bow bears the face of a tiger and looks awesome. He possesses a long crown with a big flower at he end decorated with glittering peacock feathers. He has a string of beads on the neck, feathers of 'ara' (a bird with brown feathers found in lake Chilka) on his arms, a mirror and a string of beads on his wrist, flags on the arrows, handkerchief tied to the hands, a small bell attached to the thigh.

He smears his body with 'rama raja' (a powder of yellow colour) to save himself from the scorching heat of summer. He decorates his forehead with vermilion. He wears an artificial beard and moustache. Dressed up he looks very ferocious. This dance is not accompanied by any song.

Ghumra Dance

The 'Ghumra' - a kind of drum of the size of a pitcher - produces a deep musical sound. The drummer ties the rope of the ghumra round his neck, makes it hang and plays on it, sings and dances to its tune at social functions like marriages or any religious festival. Sometimes a competition is held between two parties. Each party consists of twenty to twenty-five men and the dance goes on the whole night. Ghumra is prevalent among the 'Sahara' and other Aborigines and Harijans and songs have love as their main theme. The other forms of folk dance like 'Humo', 'Bauli', 'Jhulki', 'Jamudali', 'Mayalajar', 'Gunjikata', 'Rasarkeli' and 'Puchi' are prevalent among the Oriyas and Aborigines of Orissa.

20

Tribal Dances of Punjab

FOLK DANCE

Folk-dances of the Punjab virtually hold a mirror to the characteristic Punjabi manliness, fortitude, forthrightness and gaiety. The dances are down-to-earth and devoid of all superficiality or sophistication.

Folk-dances are not bound by any rigid rule. They are an expression of emotions through physical movements. The dancer is free to synchronise any emotion with a gesture that he finds appropriate. The folk dancer does not need any special dress or make-up. The dancers are basically so simple that virtually no preparation is required for them.

The folk-dances are secular in character. Members of different sects and creeds, irrespective of their faiths, get together and dance. The main object of the dances are fun and entertainment. The musical instrument dhol (drum) is an essential in the folk-dances.

The men and women do not dance together. They form separate groups. Folk dances are generally not the same for men and women but some dances are common to both. Bhangra is the men's dance and Giddha is the women's dance. Bhangra and Giddha are the most popular folk-dances of the Punjab.

Bhangra

Bhangra is the favourite dance of the Punjabi villager. It is a dance of stamina in sheer force and tempo. This ancient dance is associated with the ripening of the harvest. The origin of this is associated with fertility rites.

This dance is performed on Baisakhi when harvesting is over and fairs are held all over the Punjab. It can also be performed without any let or hindrance at any other social occasion of importance.

No particular form of dress is indicated for Bhangra. For maintaining unifromity, the dancers wear shirts with loose sleeves, stiff-starched long-cloth tahmats (loose loin cloth reaching up to the ankles) and bright black, red, green or yellow waist-coasts. A bright strip over the turban is often regarded as a must. Tiny bells are sometimes tied over the ankles.

Bhangra is danced to the accompaniment of dhol and rhythmic clapping. The drummer stands at the centre and the dancers stand in a circle around him. At the beat of the drum, they proceed first with a slow movement of the feet then a rhythmic wriggling of the body and after the shaking of the shoulders they start strutting in rhythm. The tempo increases as the beat of the drum becomes more and more exciting. The physical movements in twist and turn take the drumming and dance to a fine climax.

The drummer and the dancers all reaching a stage of swinging ecstasy where sound and movements merge into each other. The flow of the rhythm is interspersed with chants of "Hoy, Hoy" and "Balle, Balle" by the dancers. There are short pauses in between. At each pause when the drumming ceases one of the dancers comes forward, puts one hand on his ear lifts the other and sings a Boli. As soon as he comes to the end of it, dancing is resumed. The dancers must keep the rhythm and increase or decrease the tempo in accordance with the beat of the drum.

Sometimes young men divide themselves competitively into pairs, each pair performing in its turn while the rest remain in a circle. The gestures are full of vigour that they are difficult to sustain over long periods. So when a pair exhausts itself, it goes back to the ring and another pair comes forward to take its places. This may go on for hours.

With the passage of time Bhangra, is losing its gruffness and its movements are tending to become more and more sophisticated. The Bhangra which is danced on Republic Day and in the films is quite different from the one danced in villages by the unsophisticated people.

Giddha

Giddha is the folk-dance par excellence of women. It has almost the same intensity as Bhangra. It leaves plenty of margin for the depiction of feminine grace and elasticity. Women perform this dance mainly on festive and social occasions especially marriages. In Malwa, the Giddha performed during marriages is called 'Viyahula Giddha'. Hard worked village women sometimes get together on moonlit nights and dance in tune with nature. It is customary in the Punjab to celebrate Teeyan in the month of Sawan.

The festival lasts from the 3rd lunar day in the month to full moon. Fairs are held at many places, swings are put up and girls swing and dance to their heart's content. At such times Giddha is performed under a peepal or banyan tree. The rainy season is also called the season of Giddha because the drops of rain and the dark clouds inspire the girls to dance out their pent-up feelings as nothing else can. Giddha performed during Teeyan is called 'Teeyan Giddha'. For young girls whether married or unmarried it is an occasion to look forward to.

The newly-married ones yearn to come to their parental homes during these days.

Giddha is danced in a circle. The girls form a ring. One of them taking up a small drum (dholki) and sitting in the centre. If a dholki is not available an earthen pitcher is substituted. The deserved rhythm is produced by striking it with a pebble. The starting procedure is the same as in Bhangra. One girl comes forward and sings a boli. As she comes to the end of it, the others pick up the refrain and join. As the dance proceeds they sing more and more spiritedly, keeping time by clapping. The girls dance in twos. The dance is stylistically simple, the jingle of the bells the thumping of the feet and the beat of the drum creating an enchanting atmosphere.

Giddha is not performed according to any cut-and-dried rule but harmony is the essence in such movements as swinging and twisting the body, shaking the shoulders, bending to a double and clapping. Sometimes four young girls perform Kikli in group of two's. Girls performing Giddha indicate through gestures the various phases of the life of a Punjabi woman spinning, fetching water from the well and grinding.

Whichever phase they portray, they sing with it an appropriate boli. Mimicry is very popular in Giddha. One girl may play an aged bridegroom and another his young bride or one may play a quarrelsome sister-in-law and another a humble bride. All this gives women a chance to give uninhibited expression to their pent-up feelings.

Sammi

This is a popular dance of Sandal Bar. This is a women's dance and like the Giddha it is danced in a circle. The dancers stand in a ring and swing their hands bringing them up from the sides, right in front, up to the chest and clap. They take the hands down in accordance with a rhythm and a system and clap again.

Repeating this gesture, they bend forward and clap again and go round and round in a circle, as the rhythm is maintained with the beat of the feet. Various kinds of swinging movements are performed with the arms.

This is a very simple dance. Most of the gestures and confined to the movements of the arms, clicking and clapping. No instrument is required as an accompaniment to this dance. Rhythm is kept up with the beating of feet and clapping. The dance is named after the young heroine of a legend, Sammi, who was madly in love and used to sing and dance as best she could for the sake of her lover.

Kikli

Kikli is generally popular with the younger girls. They form pairs and then the two girls of each pair stand opposite each other holding each other's hands crosswise.

Then they lift their heels and swing round and round on their toes. The movements gets faster and faster, the upper part of the body bends backward and the arms remain fully stretched.

As the spinning gathers momentum, it creates an ecstasy and the girls go on and on till they reach the point of exhaustion. Even though they move very fast, they are very careful to maintain rhythm and keep singing various kinds of songs about the mother, the father, the brother, the mother-in-law and about various incidents connected with daily life.

Luddi and Jhumar are also famous dances especially for auspicious occasions. Luddi is generally danced to celebrate a victory. Dancers lift both arms, hop on one foot and move in a circle, swinging their bodies and shaking their shoulders. Though no songs are sung with Luddi, it is a dance bursting with enthusiasm.

Jhumar

The Jhumar is a folk dance of the harvest season. Although it shares many features with the Bhangra, it can be clearly distinguished from the latter on account of its thematic content and its emphasis on recreating the gaits of animals and birds. In the Bhangra, there is not attempt to show the movements of sowing and reaping the harvest; in the Jhumar all the functions of daily life are recreated and the pairs of dancers who come into the central area, often imitate the movements of the animals they rear. Two men become bullocks of the field, a third plough and the fourth a farmer. The gaits of the animals, the ploughing of the field, sowing of the seeds and harvesting are shown step by step. The crops are cut and then the dancers again rejoin into a circle and dance very much in the manner as of the Bhangra.

Karthi

Karthi is the only mixed dance of men and women, which used to be more popular in the hills, than in the plains. While the Bhangra and the Jhumar are not preceded by any ritual to a deity, in the Karthi, offerings are first made to a deity, at a harvest time. This is followed by women leading the processions and singing songs.

The men follow, and then a circle is formed with men and women alternating and linking hands. The accompanying songs are sentimental, and tell of battles fought and victories won, of the union and quarrels of lovers. The tempo of the Karthi is a slower than the tempo of the other two dances.

There is much clapping of hands both singly and in pairs. While no wind instruments are used in the Bhangra and the Jhumar, a folk Shenai and other wind instruments are in evidence in the Karthi.

21

Tribal Dances of Rajasthan

REGIONAL DANCE FORMS

Folk dances of Rajasthan has been classified according to the three natural division of the region - hilly, desert and eastern plain including Shekhawati.

The Hilly Region

The hilly areas inhabited by Bhils and Meenas are known for community songs and dances. Songs and dance are an integral part of their life. The dances are participated in by both men and women without any reservation. The dances of the Bhils and Meenas are many and are performed on festive days and during marriages.

Ghoomar is a circular dance in which men and women dance to the rhythm of the song they sing. The dance has no co-ordination with musical instruments. The tune is easy and the movements of the limbs become very agile and impressive as the dance advances.

The Ger is a community dance performed on the occasion of Holi Festival. It is only a men's dance conducted to the beating of a big drum with brass plates or Thalis. The dance becomes exciting as its tempo increases and the dancers quicken their movements, beating the sticks held in their hands.

The Ger and the Ghoomar are combined in another dance performed on Holi. It is called the Festival Ghoomar and is very spirited. Men and women come in their best attire and join this dance in gay, abandon making a very pleasing sight.

Many dances are performed on the occasion of marriages. The gait of the women in all these dances, is the characteristic feature of the Bhil dancing of Rajasthan, Madhya Pradesh and Gujarat.

The body is held relaxed, the torso is used as one unit, but there are some curved movements demanding the use of upper chest and lower waist separately. While the tempo is fast, there is little use of strong energy. There is hardly any instrumental musical accompaniment; only the song of the women forms the constant base of the dance.

Jhoria is a marriage dance. The Jhoria literally means a wooden stick. The men form one circle, the women another one and they perform a vivacious dance to the accompaniment of the dhol, shehnai and nagara.

Among the Bhils and Meenas the farewell to the bride after marriage is an important occasion for dance. The members of the bridegroom's party hold swords and dance all the way to the ringing of thalis and the madal. The women on the bride's side reciprocate holding baskets and broomsticks in their hands.

Neja is a musical dance game of the Meenas in Kherwara and Dungarpur. It is usually performed on the third day after Holi. Women erect a big pillar and tie a coconut to its top. Holding small sticks and whips, they guard it against the men-folk who try to climb it to take away the coconut. The women dancers drive them away by striking their sticks and beating their whips on their backs.

The Gauri dance of the Bhils of Udaipur is a purely religious dance performed to appease Bhairavi, their Ishladeva, during the month of Sravan and Bhadon. The dance is based on the life of Siva and lasts from morning till evening. During the rainy season, the Bhils remain out of their homes for a month, and utilize their outing to exhibit their dancing feats which are related to the stories of 'Bhoodhia', an epithet of Siva. This dance reminds one of the Kathakali of south India with its colour and variety. The episodes of Bhiyanwad, Banjara, Khadlia Bhoot and the tiger-boar bout lend much charm and effect to the Gauri.

The Banjaras are a nomadic tribe of Rajasthan who used to carry all sorts of goods from one place to another on their bullock carts. They are found of dancing. Their women's dresses are pretty and colourful and they usually dance in couples. The Gangaur festival is the biggest occasion for dancing and the Banjaras dance to the beating of the dholak. In the absence of the dholak they create music by beating thalis and Katoris.

The Bagarias are the another nomadic tribe. They are the sellers of broomsticks and mendicants. The men do not dance but women perform attractive dances set to tuneful music. The instrument used is generally the Chang. Bagara women go from door to door begging and dancing.

The Garasias, a hill tribe like Bhils and Meenas celebrate the Gangaur and Holi festivals with community dancing. The Garva is a peasant dance of Gangaur in which only women take part. The Valar is another Gangaur dance in which both men and women join. Uniformity of movement in the large group of dancers and agility are the notable features of this dance. In the Ger dance of Garasias, women are not allowed to participate.

The dancers hold sticks or dandis and rhythm is kept with a big drum and a thali. It is a Holi dance full of life and vigour. Another Holi dance of Garasias is the Chang. One person plays on the chang and many dancers holding sticks in their hands move and jump in the disorderly crowd. The peculiarity of the dance lies in the rhythmic jumps and leaps of the dancers who sing romantic but obscene songs. Women do not join the dance but they accompany the jumping male dancers with songs.

The Kalbelias are snake-charmers traditionally wedded to music and dance. Their dances are performed singly and sometimes in couples, the Kalbelia and his wife dance to boost their income.

Their popular dances are Indoni, Shankaria and Panihari. Both Indoni and Panihari are popular folk songs and the dances are based on them. Indoni is a group dance performed in a circle. The Poongi and Khanjair are the instruments which keep the rhythm. The costumes of the snake-charmer's wives, embroidered and colourful lend gaiety to the dance.

The Shankaria is danced by couple. It is based on a love story and its is very artistic in this movement. The Panihari is also performed by a couple and casts a spell of its own on the audience.

The Adbhopas of Mewar live in appalling proverb. Their women are gifted with melodious voices and sing when begging for alms and dance too as a professional entertainers.

The Bhavais is a community of musicians and dancers include Jats, Charmars, Raigars, Bhils, Meenas and Kumhars within their fold. Their dances are physically vigorous and help to keep the dancers fit. Their women do not join them in the dance to entertain the Yajmans Patrons.

The Desert Region

The Ghoomar also called Jhumar may be described as the national dance of the women of Rajasthan. It is a collective dance in which hundreds of women can join and dance in giant circle. It is performed on festive days in middle-class families in Udaipur, Jodhpur and Kota Bundi areas. In Udaipur, it resembles the Garva of neighbouring Gujarat and is very musical. In Jodhpur, the movement of the limbs are jerky. The Ghoomar of Kota Bundi is very lively and impressive. The tune of the song which accompanies this dance is melodious and catchy.

The fire-dance of the Siddha Jats of Bikaner is remarkable for its sensational and awe-inspiring impact. Maharaja Ganga Singh of Bikaner was a great patron of the fire dancers who inhabit Katriasar, Bhamlu, Dikamdesar and other villages. The fire dancers make a born-fire to the beating of drums, the playing of the bher and the singing of a song. Inspired by tumultuous music, the dancers, including old men and even children jump on to the fire and dance over it. As the dance, gathers tempo, they lift burning coals and throw them on others but do jot cause any injury. The dance lasts half an hour, it does not leave burns on the dancers.

The drum dancers of Jalore are professionals. It is performed during marriages, this male dance is a synthesis of various folk dances. Four or five drums are beaten simultaneously and one of the dancers holds a sword between his teeth, another carries sticks in his hands, a third swings handkerchiefs from his arms and the remaining simply make movements to the rhythm of the dance.

The Teratali is a peculiar dance-form of the desert and Deedwana and Pokaran are its centres. Those who practices this dance-form are known as Kamads and the party usually consists of two men and two women. The men play the ektara and sing, while the women produce musical notes from the manjiras tied to various parts of their bodies. The postures and the twists of the body necessary to extract musical rings from the manjira are very difficult to perform.

The Kachhi Ghori dance of marwar performed to the beat of the dhol and turhi by four or five dancers during marriage, presents a scene of warriors riding horses.

The dancers of the Kan-Gujari are mendicants who describe themselves as incarnations of Radha-Krishna. They beg from door to door, singing to the tunes of the Ravanhattya and dancing with highly artistic movements.

The Bhopas are a minstrel community divided into five sects. They also dance and Bhopas of Gogaji, Mataji and Bhaironji go into such ecstasy while dancing that they sometimes become unconscious.

Eastern Region

The eastern part of Rajasthan adjoins the Braj region of Uttar Pradesh and probably because of this affinity retains a rich tradition of Ras-Lila, Ram-Lila, Nautanki and other dance forms.

The community dance of Gindar is a night-long affair on the occasion of Holi. It is a democratic dance in which caste Hindus and Harijans join hands in a circle in the centre of which the nagara is played on a wooden platform. Starting on a low note, the nagaras reach a high pitch and with every beat of the nagara, the dancers strike their sticks and ring ghungroos tied to their legs.

The Kanjars and the Sansis are two ex-criminal tribes of Rajasthan whose women are good dancers. The dancers of the Sansi women are disorderly, individualistic and vulgour and they perform them for every meagre payment.

The Gher Ghemur of the Sansis is the simplest of the dances, both in content and form. It begins with a slow movement where men and women first dance in two separate lines and then form a circle with man and women alternately. The tempo of the dance increases gradually to a point where each person has both a rotating movements around his own axis, as also a revolving movement along the circumference of the circle. The hip movements are the most characteristic feature of this dance. There is both instrumental and vocal music accompaniment to this dance. The dance is vigorous and there are no languorous movements.

The Kanjar women, though Muslim but look life Hindus and decorate their bodies with many kinds of cheap metal ornaments and beads. They sing well and dance exuberantly. Their males play on the chang and dholak. One of their dances is performed with lathis. They also dance for a living on festivals life Holi and Diwali.

The dances of the Nayaks, Chamars and Mehtars are very attractive and full of life and vitality.

The Kachhi Ghori dance in eastern Rajasthan is virtually a battle-dance in which riders of cloth or paper' horses' moving in a circle strike blows at each other and demonstrate the use of sword and the shield. As the name implies, the dance is a presentation of horse-riding. The horse used in the dance is made of two small bamboo sticks with two baskets tied to each end.

An artistically prepared head of a horse is fixed to one of the baskets and a bunch of flex-fibre to the other. The dancer, dressed as a bridegroom in flowing costume and with sword in hand "adjusts the horse" on his waist in such a way as to create a realistic effect.

Movements are jerky and angular. These dancers are called in to perform at marriages. In the Shekhawati area, the Kachhi Ghori dancers of Ganeri, Nechwa and Ramgarh are well known.

Geeder is danced by the tribes of the Shekhawati area. It begins fifteen days before Holi. In this, only men take part. Drums are kept on a raised platform and the dancers form circles. Sticks are also used. It resembles the Gher in many ways. In this and other dances, we observe the coalescing of the levels of agricultural functions and myths.

Costumes of the Dancers

The costumes of the dancers of Rajasthan either tribal or urban society, have many common elements. The closely gathered ghagra (skirt) is common to all the tribes and castes of Rajasthan. The design and the type of the skirt varies from region to region and the kind of material used also changes from level to level but bright-coloured prints are common; particular prints are earmarked for special groups. The women wear long-sleeved cholis and have very large beautifully printed dupattas.

The ornaments are both silver and gold. The Bhil tribes use silver, but the sophisticated women of the aristocracy prefer gold ornaments. A characteristic feature of the head ornament is the bolda which is a gold ornament with stones and is worn in the centre of the forehead; this is also a common ornament for the lowliest and the highest.

The characteristic costume of the men consists of a tightly worn dhoti with a traditional bandi and a turban. Although the type of the dhoti as also the long-sleeved bandis vary from region to region in Rajasthan, the manner of draping is common to practically all the communities of Rajasthan.

22

Tribal Dances of Sikkim

Khang-chen-dzod-nga Dance: The two day festival of dance performed during the worship of snowy range of Kanchanjunga (Khang-chen-dzod-nga) is a dance peculiar to Sikkim alone. It is celebrated in September. The third Chogyal of Sikkim, Chador Namgyal (1686-1716) introduced this dance about two and a half centuries ago as a result of a vision.

Kanchendzonga is portrayed as a fiery red - countenanced deity with a crown of five skulls, riding the mythical snow lion and holding aloft the banner of victory. Esoteric masks, flashing silks, opulent brocades and embroidered boots are the costumes of the dancers.

The dancers are all male. In this warrior Dance the warlike pomp and panoply, the war deity resplendent the flaming robes, the fantastic Snow lion, comprise the essence of the dance. This mask dance is termed as Singhi Dance i.e. Lion Dance by Nepalese. They visualise the ferocious god of Kanchanjunga riding over a lion and hence call this dance as Singhi Dance.

Black Hat (Kali topi) Dance: On Lossoong, the Sikkimese New Year Day, Black Hat (kali topi) Dance demonstrating the triumph of good over evil is demonstrated. This masked dance is also performed by male dancers mostly the Lamas. The dance revives the old story which narrates that about twelve centuries ago King Land-Darma was slain for suppressing Buddhism in Tibet. The king was slain by a

Lama wearing a fantastic black robe lined with white and riding a white horse blackened with soot.

Other dances are 'Bara Singha Dance (the Stag dance) and Kankal Dance (the Skeleton Dance) and folk dances like, the Limbus celebrating a good harvest. There are some soft rhythm dances too in which women can participate. The Tamang (Dampu Dance)and Maruni dances (Nepali Dance) are such in which a couple wavering lighted tapers on their open palms participate. The Limbus perform the Dhol Dance after harvesting their paddy crop. Lepcha people also perform a group dance after harvests. The Lepcha folk dances are quite bristle and Gay. The Sikkimese dances find their roots in the traditional culture seasonal cycles of this fabled Himalayan state.

23

Tribal Dances of Tamilnadu

Bharathanatyam, the most famous classical dance of India originated in Tamil Nadu. The folk dances are the following

Kolattam

Kolattam, derived from Kol(a small stick), and Attam (play) is the name of a charming Tamil dance practiced by groups of young girls. A festival connected with this art has both a cultural and a religious significance. According to legends, once there lived an Asura called Basavasura who could not be controlled by anybody. Some girls joined together in a group, went to this Asura and played Kolattam with charming music. The Asura was so pleased with the divine music and grace of the girls, that he gave up all his evil designs. This has since been celebrated as Kolatta Jothrai in a number of places in Tamil Nadu.

'Basava' - the bull, the personification of Shiva is the centre of the Kolattam festival, commencing every year on the new moon day of the October-November and ending on the full moon day. Daily, girls take their bath early in the morning in the holy rivers and they pick up a handful of grass and water in a small container and return to the place where they have installed the clay idol of Basava.

The girls then offer the grass to lord Basava, place the water near the bull and worship. While playing Kolattam the girls visit some houses in the village to play Kolattam in each house. On the purnima day, scheduled for the immersion of Basava, the girls dressed in new clothes placing the Basava in a decorated palanquin ultimately immerse it in a river. In every stage of the festival, each girl has one stick in each of her hands and the stick in the hand of each girl is struck against those of the other girls in rotation, producing beautiful music.

KAVADI

Lord Muruga or Subrahmanya, the son of Lord Shiva, has annihilated all the evil forces of demons. He is said to be reside in six embattled field-camps called Padaiveedus. Palani and Thirupparakundram in Madurai district are two such holy places. They are hillocks described in mythology as carried by a giant called Idumban slung on the two ends of a pole placed on his shoulder.

This Idumban became one of the principal devotees of Lord Subrahmanya. He has a shrine half-way up the Palani hill and receives the first honours from all devotees proceeding to worship Subrahmanya. Actually the worship of Lord Subrahmanya without paying homage to Idumban is considered ineffective. The carrying of Kavadi by pilgrims is symbolic of Idumban carrying the hillocks, the abodes of the Lord slung on a pole.

There are several kinds of Kavadis- the milk and rose-water Kavadi being the principal ones. The central shaft of the semi-circular wooden structure is placed on the shoulders and the pilgrims dressed in yellow costume and decorated with garlands, undergoing many privations to fulfill vows. They dance their way through the streets and up the hillock under the hypnotic music provided by the drum, the pipes and the tom-tom.

It is a Tandava as opposed to the Lasya form of dance. Extreme devotion prompts some Kavadi dancers to disfigure their lips. The lower lip is pierced through for the insertion of a copper or brass ring, often with a view to maintain silence.

The dancers subject themselves to rigorous austerities and try to get rid of their ego, anger, lust and other vices. They dance to the tunes of Kavadi-c-cindu, sung by admiring groups of devotees who follow the dancers. The divine songs are rendered in charming music by a trained singer and repeated by others in chorus and the emotion-chocked dancer goes into raptures hearing them. Sometimes they react by shifting the Kavadi over their shoulder, head, nose etc. in see-saw position displaying great artistry with many a pose and movement in rhythm, unaided by hands.

Kavadi-c-cindu, a peculiar folk art of Tamil genius has blossomed into a literary and technically brilliant form. It gives a lilting tune and inspiration to listeners and relieves the bearer of the Avid of physical pain. It is also called Vazhinadai-cindu. It is sung by pilgrims while trekking long distances, to forget the tedium.

The Kavadi-c-cindu is sung not only by pilgrims on the march but also in temples. In some temples, it is sung on the last day of Navarathri in different metres. In Tiruchendur and in Palani, the cindus are sung with Nadaswaram before the deity starts in procession. These songs describe the romantic relationship of Muruga to Valli.

Karakam Dance

Karakam is a folk art developed along with the cult of Mariamman. It is of two varieties- the religious and the professional. The religious type is called Sakti Karakam. A small pot is filled with water and sealed with a coconut. Flower wreaths decorate it and a lime fruit is placed at the top of the Karakam. The temple priest or his nominee carries it with great ceremony and sentimental attachment since this is one of their hereditary privileges.

The professional type is known as Attak Karakam and is performed anywhere by anyone with necessary practice and skill. It is one of the Tamil Nadu's regular showpieces at the republic day floats in New Delhi every year.

The Attak Karakam or balancing of the pot on the head is accompanied by peculiar musical instruments called Pampadi, Urumi, Thavil, Nadaswaram and Thamukku which are among the distinctive components of Tamil music. The Karakam dancers wear a close fitting dress and look like warriors. They remind one of the Kudak-Koothu dancers described in the literary work, Chilappadikaram.

The word Karakam denotes a pot or kumbham filled with sacred water for purificatory purposes. During ordinary rituals all the seas of Varuna, the Lord of rains and the seven sacred rivers are supposed to be attracted and confined in the Karakam and released only when the final ablution is performed and the water is poured or sprinkled over the heads of the worshippers.

In Tirunelveli district, Karakam is also called Amman Kondadi or a way of eliciting the blessing of the goddess.

The Karakam dancer smears his bare body with holy ash and sandal paste and wears a short skirt. On his head, he balances a pot filled with uncooked rice, surmounted by a tall conical bamboo frame, covered with flowers. He starts from a holy spot or a square and goes to the temple in a procession. Dancing with quick steps, he brandishes a sword or a staff while two people beat the drum and blow on a long pipe. From a slow tempo, the dance rises to delirious frenzy, when the dancer becomes oblivious of himself. Though he tumbles and leaps, he somehow retains the pot on his head without touching it. Background music is provided by Nayyandi Melam.

Puravai Attam

Puravai Attam also known as Poikkal Kuthirai, is a dummy horse show. The dummy horse is made of jute, cardboard, paper, and glass. The show is performed by men as well as women.

The main attraction is the richly decorated cardboard horse. The dancer uses this as his dress. He gets into it through the holes made therein and looks as if he is riding on horse back. Wooden stilts are tied to the dancers feet and these can be successfully used only after months of experience. The purpose of using the stilts is to prevent the dancer from being harmed by snakes or scorpions.

This dance is performed by a pair of dancers impersonating a king and queen. Sometimes, they indulge in acrobatics and they entertain the folk for hours together.

The dummy-horse show is one of the chief attractions in the republic day festivities at New Delhi and folk artists are sent from Tamil Nadu every year to perform this show.

Arayar Natanam

Arayar Natanam is enacted in December-January in Shrirangam and other Shri Vaishnava temples by groups of musicians and a dancer who are engaged to recite the sacred hymns called the Thiruvaimozhi.

This class of choirists called Arayar or Chanters are on the temple staff receiving allowances and perquisites. They wear a uniform which includes a Kireetam or special conical cap as their badge during the chanting. While chanting the hymns, they also use a pair of cymbals made of bell-metal. One of them assumes the postures. In between their recitations, they utter the glory of the presiding deity by singing Kondattam.

The Araya's practice a certain esoteric system of dance wherein the postures are conventional and present situations associated with lord Krishna's Juvenile Pranks.

Podikazhi Attam

Podikazhi Attam is a popular dance among the fishermen of the coastal villages near Pondichery during the festival of their favourite deity Muruga. Eight to sixteen men in their traditional costumes perform the dance to the accompaniment of drums, and music is performed mostly by women.

Navasandhi

Navasandhi meaning nine directions is a dance

performed to the accompaniment of music at the flag-hoisting ceremony, which heralds the annual festival of the temple at Tiruchendur. Several other dance traditions have been noticed in a number of temples in Tamil Nadu. The dances performed by the Palanquin-bearers of the Lord are other variations of the drama tradition combining music and dance.

Kuravaik-Koothu

This is a type of dance in which seven girls form a circle clapping one other's hand. This dance is referred to as Aichiyar Kuravai or the dance of the cowherd women in Chilappadikaram.

This dance has a peculiar musical significance. The seven notes of the musical scale are arranged in a circle and the seven girls are called by the names of the seven musical notes viz Kural, Tattam, Kalikkilae. The Achoponga Folk dance is a remnant of this defunct dance. In this dance, a number of girls form a circle and do simple rhythmic movements, singing and clapping their hands according to the rhythm.

Kazhaikoothu

This is a dance performed by standing on bamboo poles. A specimen of this occurs in bas-relief sculptured in the Sri Andal Temple at Srivilliputhur. The dancer balances himself standing on two poles, each two meters long, dancing to the accompaniment of a two-faced drum played by his wife.

Kummi

In Kummi, girls sing several songs. Kummi consist of common Kummi and the Oyil Kummi. In the common Kummi, the dancers are rhythmical and the girls dance in different postures. The rhythm of both dance and music delights the audience. The word Kummi is said to be derived from Kommai and means to 'dance with clapping of hands' to time and singing poems in a metre adopted to Kummi dance.

Oyil Kummi

Oyil Kummi or Oyil Attam is performed by large groups of men wearing bells on their feet and narrating mythological stories. The invocation song prays to gods and also instructs the participants to give adequate space for the movement of the neighbours legs and prevent their coming into physical contact.

Bommalattam or Pavakkuthu

This is puppet dance and this art form is used to spread religious stories. Simple folk believe that it is auspicious to have this performance in their village and that its performance will ward off evil spirits/epidemics and bring prosperity. The main themes are the stories from the Ramayana, the Mahabharatha and the Bhagavatha. This show is manipulated by strings and iron rods suspended from above. The stage is so setup that the puppets alone are seen through an opening roughly about four metres in height. The puppets are moved by skilled and experienced players who stand behind, unseen by the audience. The puppets are tied to the player's hand with black strings which are not visible.

The performance usually begins at 10 pm. and is over by about 4 am, the following morning it is continued for a week or ten days. On either side of the stage big earthen castor oil lamps are placed. The screen is a big black cloth about three metres high. In front of this curtain, the puppet make their appearance.

When the chandramati puppet and the dancing puppet appear, the manipulators behind the curtains have themselves to do all the bodily movements and dancing. Their legs and arms have full work. The scenes in which chandramati tears her garland to pieces and laments on the cremation ground are great attractions.

Leather puppet show

The leather puppet show introduced from Maharashtra to Thanjavur is sometimes held in Tamil Nadu. These puppets are made of thin goat skin carefully cured to make them translucent. They are cut and joined in such a way that the limbs can be moved. They are painted with ordinary dry and deep colours as men, women, gods, goddess, demons and animals. Many of them being as tall as human beings. Operated from below, they are made to gesticulate, move and dance with considerable skill.

24

Tribal Dances of West Bengal

In ancient Bengal, dancing was popular entertainment. Courtesans and temple girls (devadasis) were required to be proficient in the art of dance prescribed by Bharata in his 'Natysastra'. Popular forms of dancing were rendered at mundane celebrations and on other occasions by low-caste tribes Nats and Domnis (women of the Dom caste) who practiced dancing and singing as hereditary professions. In the Middle ages, probably the institution of temple girls become obsolescent and class dancing was limited to courtesans. As a result dancing came to be looked down up on in respectable society.

Rabindranath Tagore has the credit of rehabilitating dancing as a fine art to be learnt by young as a part of their education. In his school at Santiniketan and later in his university Viswabharati, he provided ample facilities for training in these acquirements. He had profound admiration for the rich treasure of the classical dances of India but he thought these required too rigid a discipline and too elaborate a training to be feasible for the general public. He therefore introduced a simple course of instruction in dancing to his songs of the seasons.

By 1926 this developed into a flexible system compounding elements of Bharatnatyam, Manipuri, Kathak, Kathakali and folk styles. This creative system was very well received by the Bengali public and has since grown into a major cultural activity. A large number of institutions teaching the elements of classical dances and presenting ballet compositions have come into existence in Calcutta and the towns. Evolution of an Indian ballet tradition has been the quest of institution presided over by Udayashankar, who well versed in European ballet made his debut in this field in 1929 and has made Calcutta his headquarters since over a decades ago. During the last twenty five years the new dance movement has made considerable progress not only in West Bengal but also other parts of India and Bangladesh.

The Santals inhabiting the plateau Fringe have their own system of group dancing to the accompaniment of song, the flute and Madal (a minor drum) to express their joy of life. It is full-blooded and exuberant but notably free from vulgarity or obscenity.

CHHAU DANCE

The Chhau dance of Purulia district is a sophisticated dance system in Bengal. The Chhau dance is a mask dance. There is no Chhau without mask. This dance is usually performed by male dancers. Chhau dance of Purulia has some characteristics of primitive ritualistic dance in its vigour, style and musical accompaniment mainly the drum. The symbols were once used as facial painting or body painting by dancers who were thus recognized as personifying the characters they stimulated and the masks appeared later.

The best Chhau dance groups or parties are located within Baghmundi P.S. They are the best because of their traditional vigorous and heroic style of performance. The other groups (Domordi-group, Birgram-group, Madla-group etc) are more sophisticated and refined both in their themes and dance-styles. The Chorda-group of dancers are not only best performs of heroic Pauranic themes, but also are very much selective about such themes for their performance. Chhau mask dance is predominantly a Bhumij art. All the majority of dancer are Bhumji.

Makara Sankranti is an important festival in all parts of Bengal. The Tusu Parab is held in Birbhum on this occasion. Groups of young girls gather every evening throughout the month of Pousa (December-January) and sing songs which have been termed by the generic term Tusu. On the day of Makara Sankranti the groups go out of the village to a nearby tank or river with the goddess Tusu symbolized in small clay figurines or sometimes merely as cow-dung balls.

After a sacred bath they return to worship and make offerings of rice to the deity. Different groups meet, sing songs near the river-bank or the pond and compete with each other. The songs are accompanied by simple group movements: there is no other accompaniment. The men also have their particular songs and dances for the occasion and these are known as the Bhaduriya Saila. The dance content is more predominant here: men dance in circles clock-wise and anti-clockwise.

In Chaitra, another type of composition known as the Jhumar is sung and danced. Jhumar can be sung and danced by only one men and women or both depending upon the particular occasion. The Jhumar at Chaitra is a typical men's dance which is accompanied by drum and cymbals. At time of the transplanting of the paddy only women sing and dance the Jhumar. This is then known as the Ashariya Jhumar. Into the agricultural songs of transplanting paddy was impregnated the theme of the love of Radha and Krishna and other stories of mystical union. The basic tune of the Jhumars remained more or less the same. The development of the Jhumar provides an interesting instance of an old form absorbing a new content.

The agricultural dances have gradually given place to dances which are purely devotional or religious in character. Practically each different sect has its own music and dances. The worshippers of Shakti, dance in the Chandi mandir of Siva, in the dance hall called Gambhira and those of Vishnu in the Natmandir. All these pavilions are specially constructed for the dance in front of the shrine.

The Gambhira festival is held on this day. So also is the Kesvar where Siva is worshipped. Gazan dance is performed by men dressed in saffron robes who carry a Dhanuchi (incensed burners). This is exclusively performed by men; the musical accompaniment is provided by decorated drums and brass gongs (Kanshi).

The ballad singers, the boatmen, the fishermen and the professional musician dancers, actors, acrobats and even jugglers have their distinctive songs and dances. A characteristic feature of these is the musical accompaniment which consists of a one stringed instrument called the ektara. The dance movements are by and large, restricted to short sequences which intersperse the singing.

The footwork is elementary, but the movement of the pelvic griddle is difficult and characteristic. It is freely used by men singing the songs to indicate a dramatic moment.

The Raibense dance of Birbhium district is a traditional system with a martial motif. The dancers rhythmically flourish staves as they execute vigorous steps. These dances have their strict codes and disciplines unlike the crude and vulgar exhibitionism of the Domnis whose vogue has dimnished greatly. The dances of the Raibenshes of Burdwan and Birbhum seem to be the last surviving vestiges of war-like traditions.

The technique of the dances is so vigorous that there has been a new interest in teaching these dances to educated boys and girls of urban centres specially by the Bratachari organisation. Dance is a series of vigorous physical exercises, in which the erect torso has an important part to play. The dancers begin in a single file and then make a circle. Hops, jumps and circles are characteristic. Skills with the shield and the spear and the trishul are common. A percussion instrument accompanies the dance.

Theatre

Jatra, is the traditional theatre form of Bengal. The Jatra is performed by travelling troupes under the management of a man called Adhikari. Although, originally the Jatra had only the themes of Radha and Krishna, today Jatras are written and performed by writers and dramatists of rural and urban centres.

25

Banjara: The Tribal Gypsies of India, A Source of Nomadic Tribal Bellydance

Cholis are significantly more used in Tribal belly dance as coined bras. Cholis organically come from India and became very popular among the American Tribal Style and middle eastern tribal style costuming.

The ancient art of middle eastern dance has a long and colorful history. It began with the many fertility cults of the ancient world, and in the temples of ancient India. The existence of various nomadic groups of professional entertainers, and groups specifically identified with Gypsies (Rom), provided for the cross-culturation and transmission of these dances.

The history of middle eastern dance is intertwined with that of Gypsies, in their various guises in each country they travelled through. They came from India and spread through Persia, Turkey, Arabia, Egypt, Greece, and through much of Europe. To this day, many nomadic women in the Near East bear hand and ankle tattoos thought to be Gypsy in design, often a universal symbol meaning a traveler. This intense tribal pride is significant in maintaining their cultural identity throughout their travels, and is characteristic of true Gypsies.

India is a vast country with many different tribes, dances and music.

Specially the dances of the Punjab, the Sind region, Rajastan and Madhya Pradesh are close to the origins of bellydance. Done by wandering gypsy tribes, the dances and costumes tell of their islamic influence or in other words: the Mughal culture.

The sophisticated art of the Hindustani gypsy dancing girls did inspire the modern-day Bollywood music and dance. Here bollywood star Aruna Irani in typical gypsy dress as Nisha, a gypsy dancer, in a movie of the sixties about a band of gypsies moving and living in a *Caravan*.

The Banjara tribe is the most colorful of any tribal group in India, the original habitants of Rajastan. Banjaras have an unique costume and embroidery style. As nomads of the Thar desert, they live in Central and of Western India. One of the dances of these tribe in Rajasthan is dancing with a jar on the head. The colorful dances of Garbha or Garbi and the Dandia are danced on the occasion of the festival of Dussehra in honour of Durga. The Mother-Godess Durga stands for the good in the world and the femininity or shakti. The dresses are ornamented with mirrors called *shishador*. Red is the dominant color. The costumes on the picture are pretty old as the use of large and irregular mirrors reflects.

The clothes and the jewelery of this particular tribe is now very popular amongst tribal bellydance style troupes. Their beautiful silver jewellery and embroidered costumes and colorful choly are a feast for the eyes. Every part of the body is ornamented with jewellery, with it's own symbolic significane. Silver is considered more precious than gold. Banjara dances differ from occasion to occasion. On the Rakhi festival, the Banjara's perform the Lehangi.

Mohiniyattam dance or dance of the enchantress, is a traditional dance from Kerala, South Indian. With hip movements and ritual expressions by the hand palm and fingers (also called mudras) it is an ancient dance done by tge Devadasis in temples.

PEOPLE AND TRIBAL DANCES

There are different tribes in the district. Their traditional dances, games and sports can be enjoyed in festive occasion.

The indigenous population is tribal and belongs to different communities. They are mainly the Mishmi, Khamtis and Singphos. Tibetan Refuges and the other sections of the population are living in the district. The indigenous people of the district co-operate any other communities in every aspect of livelihood. Till to-day the other communities appreciate all the indigenous people for their cordial and gentle behaviour. The Khamtis and the Singphos are Buddhist where as the Mishmis are the follower of typical faith, belief and practices. Monogamous is the general rules of marriage; polygamy is not a rear example for them. As a whole the occupation of the people is agriculture. They observe some worship, festivals from time to time. Singing, dancing and playing are a part and parcel of their life.

It is indeed a fact that each and every dance has got its own originality and meaning. Group dances are common along the different tribes in the district. The Mishmis mainly perform two types of dance called Buiya and Nuiya. The Khamtis Mask-dance is an attractive dance where two dancers wear shirts spotted design and on their heads masks of cock's heads are put on with its crown at the top and the Beal projecting over the foreheads. These two dancers dance like fighting cocks.

APACHE TRIBAL DANCES

The word "apache" comes from the Yuma word for "fighting-men" and from the Zuni word meaning "enemy." The Apache tribe consists of six subtribes: the Western Apache, Chiricahua, Mescalero, Jicarilla, Lipan and Kiowa. Each subtribe is from a different geographial region. They are composed of six regional groups: Western Apache - Coyotero - most of eastern Arizona which include the White

Mountain, Cibuecue, San Carlos, and Northern and Southern Tonto bands. It is possible, due to their nomadic nature, that several names were used to identify the same tribe.

The Anglo theory is the Apache Indian migrated to the Southwest from Northern Canada in the 1500's. The Apache indian history says it was the other way around, that most of the Athapaskan speaking people migrated to the North and a few stayed in their homeland. In any event, it is generally agreed that about 5,000 Apaches lived in the Southwest at the end of the 1600's.

Apaches belong to the Southern Athapascan linguistic family.

The Apache tribe occupied the mountains and plains of southern Arizona and New Mexico, and also in Mexico.

The primitive dress of the men was deerskin shirt, leggings, and moccasins. They were never without a loin-cloth. A deerskin cap with attractive symbolic ornamentation was worn. The women wore short deerskin skirts and high boot top moccasins.

Chiricahua - southwestern New Mexico, southeastern Arizona, and adjacent Mexican states of Chihuahua and Sonora - The band was the informal political unit, consisting of followers and a headman. They had no formal leader such as a tribal chief, or council, nor a decision making process. The core of the band was a "relative group," predominantly, but not nessarily, kinsmen. Named by the Spanish for the mescal cactus the Apaches used for food, drink, and fiber. The basic shelter of the Chiricahua was the domeshaped wickiup made of brush. Similar the Navajo, they also regarded coyotes, insects, and birds as having been human beings; the human race, then, but following in the tracks of those who have gone before.

Mescalero - Faraon - live east of the Rio Grande in southern New Mexico, with the Pecos River as their eastern border.

Jicarilla - Tinde - southeastern Colorado, northern New Mexico, and northwest Texas - During their zenith in the SouthWest, two divisions of the Jicarilla Apache were known: the Llanero, or "plains people," and the Hoyero, the "mountain people." They roamed from central and eastern Colorado into western Oklahoma, and as far south as Estancia, New Mexico. As a result of their eastern contacts, the Jicarilla adopted certain cultural traits of the Plains Indians, as did the Mescalero who also ranged the eastern plains. From an estimated population of 800 Jicarilla in 1845, the tribe today numbers about 1,800.

The Jicarilla (little basketmakers) are of the Athabascan language group and anthropologists say that these people came from Canada down the eastern flanks of the Rocky Mountains about 1300-1500 AD.

All tribes deny the migration theories and say that they have always been here:

The First People.

Though limited to using dogs as pack animals, the Jicarilla were the most successful raiders. When the Spaniards brought horses once again to North America (the previous horses had been eaten long before) the Jicarilla took full advantage.

They were not recognized as being distinctive from the other southern Athabascans: Chiricahuas, Navajos, Western Apaches, Mescaleros, Kiowa Apaches, and Lipans, until about 1700. Jicarilla are further identified as the plains people (Llaneros), and the mountain-valley people (Olleros) or Hoyero.

Their name for themselves is Tinde. But names that have been or are used by others than themselves are:

Mexican Spanish: Jicarilla, literally "little basket."

Navajo: Be'-xai, or Pex'-ge

Mescalero: Kinya-inde

Kiowa: Keop-tagui, "mountain Apache."

Picuris: Pi'-ke-e-wai-i-ne

Mescalero: Tashi'ne

Tesuque: Tu-sa-be'

Within the Jicarilla themselves are these smaller groups that claim certain areas as their original homes:

Dachizhozhin: site of the present Jicarilla Reservation.

Golkahin: south of Taos Pueblo.

Ketsilind: south of Taos Pueblo.

Apatsiltlizhihi: Mora.

Saitinde: around what is now Espanola.

Though all of these are in New Mexico, the Jicarilla have been all through parts of southeastern Colorado, northern New Mexico, and adjoining areas of Kansas, Oklahoma, and Texas.

Their contacts with the Spaniards began with Coronado in 1540 to 1542, perhaps as the Querechos, whom the later Spanish explorers called Vaqueros.

Hostilities began almost at first contact with the Spaniards, and though a Spanish mission was attempted near Taos in 1733, it was short-lived. Here is a general time table of the Jicarilla's relationships with the new landlords.

1853: A group of 250 Jicarilla were settled on the Puerco River, but a treaty with the governor of New Mexico was not honored by him and war broke out again.

1854: Jicarillas are defeated by the United States Army.

1870: The Jicarilla are living on the Maxwell grant in NE New Mexico, but it is sold out from under them.

1872 - 1873: The U.S. tries to move the Jicarilla to Fort Stanton.

1874: A reservation of 900 square mile is established at Tierra Amarilla, in the north of New Mexico Territory. This lasts less than four years.

1878: An Act of Congress is passed to force the Jicarilla south, they refuse, and their annuities are canceled. One version of history has called the resultant acts by the tribe as "resorting to thievery."

1880: Act of 1878 repealed, new reservation on the Navajo River.

1883: Jicarilla moved to Fort Stanton.

1887: On February 11, an Executive Order creates a reservation in the Tierra Amarilla area in northern New Mexico.

1908: A southern area is added to the reservation.

Lipan - occupy territory directly to the east of the Jicarilla

Kiowa - Gataka - long associated with the KIOWA, a Plains people, range over the southern plains of Colorado, Oklahoma, and Texas.

The Apache dwellings consisted of a dome shaped frame of cottonwood or other poles, thatched with grass. The house itself was termed, "Kowa" and the grass thatch, "Pi".

According to the Ndee from the beginning Is dzán naadleeshe', Changing Woman lived alone. One day she received inspiration to go up on a hill and build a wickiup with four poles, where the first rays of the sun would strike in the morning. Is dzán naadleeshe' went inside and lay there and as the sun came up, the sun shone between her legs. One of his rays went into her. This caused her first menstrual period. After that she became pregnant. She conceived a son and called him Nayé nazghánè; (Slayer of Monsters). Four days later she was impregnated by Water-Old Man and gave birth to Túbaadeschine (Born of the Water-Old Man). These were the first Apache people.

"The primitive Apache was a true nomad, a wandering child of Nature, whose birthright was a craving for the warpath with courage and endurance probably exceeded by no other people and with cunning beyond reckoning. Although his character is a strong mixture of courage and ferocity, the Apache is gentle and affectionate toward those with his own flesh and blood, particularly his children."

"They were always known as 'wild' Indians, and indeed their early warfare with all neighboring tribes as well as their recent persistent hostility toward our Government, which precipitated a 'war of extermination,' bear out the appropriateness of the designation."

The first intruders were the Spanish, who penetrated Apache territory in the late 1500s. The Spanish drive northward disrupted ancient Apache trade connections with neighboring tribes.

When New Mexico became a Spanish colony in 1598, hostilities increased between Spaniards and Apaches. An influx of Comanche into traditional Apache territory in the early 1700s forced the Lipan and other Apaches to move south of their main food source, the buffalo. These displaced Apaches began raiding for food.

Apache raids on settlers accompanied the American westward movement and the United States acquisition of New Mexico in 1848. The Native Americans and the United States military authorities engaged in fierce wars until all Apache tribes were eventually placed on reservations.

Most of the tribes were subdued by 1868, except for the Chiricahua, who continued their attacks until 1872, when their chief, Cochise, signed a treaty with the U.S. government and moved with his band to an Apache reservation in Arizona.

The last band of Apache raiders, led by the chief Geronimo, was hunted down in 1886 and was confined in Florida, Alabama, and finally Oklahoma Territory.

"The mescal harvest occurs in the season of new life and growth, when the call from the wild is strong in the blood, and like a class of children-for they are but grown-up children-they pour out into the wilds. From the camp where they have passed the winter they take to the trails which lead to the mescal hills."

FOOD

All Apache rely primarily on hunting of wild game and gathering of cactus fruits and other wild plant foods.

Hunting is a part of daily life - for food, clothing, shelter, blankets. Apache hunted deer, wild turkeys, jackrabbits, coyote, javelin, fox, beavers, buffalo, bears, mountain lions. There was no fishing. Eagles were hunted for their feathers. Two or three feathers were plucked from a bald eagle instead of being hunted for food.

Food was important to the Apache. Prairie dogs, snakes, turkeys, and fish in the Apache tribe were believed to be unclean so they didn't eat them. Apache boys were taught to move quickly and quietly through the forest to catch food for their family.

Every Apache male hunted. The first thing an Apache male did before hunting was greased his body with animal fat to keep out the smell of a person and make the person smell like an animal so the animals wouldn't smell the person and run away.

They exchanged buffalo hides, tallow and meat, bones that could be worked into needles and scrapers for hides, and salt from the desert with the Pueblos for pottery, cotton, blankets, turquoise, corn and other goods. But at times they simply saw what they wanted and took it. They became known among the Pueblo villages by another name, Apachu, "the enemy".

RELIGION AND CEREMONIES

The ceremonies are invariably called "dances." Among these are the rain dance, a puberty right, the sunrise dance for young women, a harvest and good crop dance, and a spirit dance.

The Apache are devoutly religious and pray on many occasions and in various ways. Recreated in the human form, Apache spirits are supposed to dwell in a land of peace and plenty, where there is neither disease or death.

SONG OF APACHE INDIANS

HUH WUHLI NICH

Ha- nam-a yo- o ya hai huh-wurt...
far on the dessert redges stands the cactus
Ka- na - hu- va muh- muhk
lo the blossoms swaying
Ka- cho-wuch-chi ka-no- ya ki-moi
to and fro the blossoms swaying, swaying

From early spring to late fall, Apache girls reaching maturity are honored by their tribe with the Sunrise Dance. This ancient ritual is a test of a girl's endurance and discipline, and a celebration of her womanhood. The Sunrise Dance typically lasts four days. During this time, the girl being honored is dancing almost constantly, to the accompaniment of over 100 songs. Although she is assisted by her godparents and friends, it's a difficult task. Each stage of the ceremony is precisely choreographed, and the girl is not permitted to falter. Beverly Malone, a member of the White Mountain Apache Tribe, is with the Fort Apache Cultural Center in Arizona. She tells us about the teachings contained in the songs and the symbols of the ceremony.

"This particular dance teaches Apache values of language, culture, food and love, prayers, respect, wisdom, cooperation, appreciation and endurance."

The Indian dancers used ankle wraps to accompany their dances. There are bells atatched to a strap of leather. When you move your leg the ankle wrap rattles and jingles. They also placed these on their knees, elbows, or ankles.

For most of the four days and nights, to songs and prayers, they dance, as well as run toward the four directions. During this time, they also participate in and conduct sacred rituals, receiving and giving both gifts and blessings, and experiencing their own capacity to heal. In the early 1900s, when the U.S. government banned Native American spiritual practices and rituals, conducting the Sunrise Ceremony was an illegal act; as a result, its practice diminished, and those ceremonies that did occur were conducted secretly.

Women play a vital role in Apache culture, and the Sunrise Dance is a way for the entire community to recognize and celebrate the meaning and value of womanhood.

"Usually the women are the main ones that are the teachers, and they are the stronghold for the family. The children claim their mom's side of the clan, and the father's clan is just like the distant family clan. It's the woman that holds the family together — that's the boss in the family."

The Apaches were hunter, farmers and seed gatherers. They knew every land feature in the plains. Apache women built irrigation ditches and planted corn. The crops were not very good, so hunters searched the land for deers, gophers, wild turkeys and lizards. The women gathered cactus fruit and acorns. The Apache loved raiding and warfare, and boys were trained for warfare since they were born. They could walk for miles without any food or water. They learned to hunt, stand guard, keep silent,and send and read smoke signals. When the boys were 15 years old they were ready to go to war. Young girls were trained by their mothers to do the household chores. The girls married very young. The daughters husband was not aloud to talk or see their mother-in-law.

Not until 1978, when the American Indian Religious Freedom Act was passed, was the Sunrise Ceremony openly re-established on most reservations. But even today, because of the expense and time involved - which also includes four days of preparation and four days of teaching and recovery - some girls celebrate for one or two days, rather than have four day ceremonies.

The families of girls entering puberty in a particular year may also sponsor joint Sunrise ceremonies, in which two or more newly menstruating girls celebrate the rites of Changing Women together.

APACHE SYMBOLS

The importance of the circle is depicted by the shape of the four sacred hoop symbols. The shape of many traditional homes is round, such as the Apache wickiup, the Navajo hogan, and the tipi of the Lakota. Religious ceremonies are performed in circular structures, such as in the hogan and the tipi. Traditional dances are also performed in a circle. The motion of the sun, moon, and stars across the sky is circular. The life paths of all creatures, including humans, are also circular.

Apache Hoop—Dee′ (San Carlos Apache) and Ndee′ (White Mountain Apache)

The Apache hoop is used in traditional ceremonies and the type of ceremony determines whether a single hoop or four hoops are used. The hoop represents the cycle of life from birth to death. It possesses special powers, which could be used, for example, to bless an individual when the hoop completely encircles the body. The hoop also has healing and protective powers.

The single Apache hoop has one of the four sacred colors of the tribe: black, green, (blue), yellow and white. These colors represent the four directions, the four seasons, and the four major divisions of the day. An eagle feather is tied at four locations on the hoop. To the Apache, and almost all tribes, the eagle is a sacred bird and its feathers are believed to have special powers.

The basket symbolizes one's realm of existence with the center opening representing one's birth into this world and the various designs representing the plains and sacred mountains among which one dwells.

The Apaches are commonly known for their incredible endurance and warfare skills. First arriving in the Southwest sometime between A.D.1000 and 1400, the Apaches carved out a home on the south side of the Rocky mountains. As early as 1540, the Apaches confronted Coronado in eastern New Mexico and were called "vaqueros." By the 1600's, they were also living in Arizona. Between 1656 and 1675, the Apaches continuously raided Spanish Settlers and Pueblo Indians in what is now known as New Mexico. In 1680, their population was approximately 5000. In 1692, the Spaniards reconquered New Mexico and the Apaches were starting to make enemies.

Cochise (Hardwood)

(Tribe : Chiricahua Apache)

c.1815-1874, chief of the Chiricahua APACHE in Arizona, noted for courage, integrity, and military skill. From 1861, when soldiers unjustly hanged some of his relatives, he warred relentlessly against the U.S. army. Peace talks in 1872 promised him a reservation on his native territory, but after he died his people were removed.

Cochise was a tall man, six feet, with broad shoulders and a commanding appearance. He never met a man his equal with a lance, and, like Crazy Horse, was never photographed. They both were buried in secret locations on their homeland.

Cochise angered by the murder of his Father-in-law, Mangas Coloradas went of a war spree.

The Cochise Stronghold, nestled in the Dragoon's canyons, was their impregnable fortress for many years. Cochise eventually signed the Broken Arrow Peace Treaty at a prominent area landmark, Council Rock. His son Naiche signaled the signing with a white flag from atop Treaty Hill.

Cochise died in 1874 of natural causes. His body was dress in his best war garments. He was decorated in war paint, and head feathers. His body was then wrapped in a brillant red blanket, and place on his horse. The horse was guided to a remote place in the Dragoons. The horse was shot and lowered into the chasm along with Cochise's gun and other arms. Lastly Cochise was lowered into the rocky cavern by lariots. The location of this burial site remains a mystery to this day.

Apache in a nine-day battle forced the Apache to move farther south. The most famous battles with the Apache happened between 1862 and 1873 when the Apache fought a bloody war against the confederate and U.S. armies. In 1873 a peace treaty was signed and the U.S. government wanted to move the Apaches to reservations. Some Apaches went peacefully but others did not.

Small factions broke out with leaders like Geronimo,Naiche and Victorio. In 1886, Geronimo and his followers were finally taken into captivity and most of the Apache renegades were moved to Fort Sill, Oklahoma where they were considered prisoners of war until 1913. Today there are over 40,000 Apaches living in reservations

As the first son of COCHISE, Taza became the leader of his father's group when Cochise died in 1874. Taza, who was also brother of NAICHE and grandson of MANGAS COLORADAS, strove to honor his father's peace agreement with the army. In 1876, he agreed to relocate his people from the Chiricahua Reservation at Apache Pass, Arizona, to the San Carlos Reservation.

However, he could not unite the various Apache bands under his leadership as Cochise had done. Consequently, GERONIMO and his followers crossed the Mexican border into the Sierra Madre of Mexico. This remote area became their base camp. In the summer of 1876, Taza joined the Apache delegation to Washington, D.C., to sue for peace. During this trip, Taza succumbed to pneumonia and was buried in the Congressional Cemetery. As a result of Taza's death, Naiche became more militant.

Geronimo {jur-ahn'-i-moh}, or Goyathlay ("one who yawns"), was born in 1829 in what is today western New Mexico, but was then still Mexican territory. He was a Bedonkohe Apache (grandson of Mahko) by birth and a Net'na during his youth and early manhood. His wife, Juh, Geronimo's cousin Ishton, and Asa Daklugie were members of the Nednhi band of the Chiricahua Apache. He was reportedly given the name Geronimo by Mexican soldiers, although few agree as to why.

As leader of the Apaches at Arispe in Sonora, he performed such daring feats that the Mexicans singled him out with the sobriquet Geronimo (Spanish for "Jerome"). Some attributed his numerous raiding successes to powers conferred by supernatural beings, including a reputed invulnerability to bullets. Geronimo's war career was linked with that of his brother-in-law, Juh, a Chiricahua chief. Although he was not a hereditary leader, Geronimo appeared so to outsiders because he often acted as spokesman for Juh, who had a speech impediment. Geronimo was the leader of the last American Indian fighting force formally to capitulate to the United States. Because he fought against such daunting odds and held out the longest, he became the most famous Apache of all.

To the pioneers and settlers of Arizona and New Mexico, he was a bloody-handed murderer and this image endured until the second half of this cent To the Apaches, Geronimo embodied the very essence of the Apache values, agressiveness, courage in the face of difficulty. These qualities inspired fear in the settlers of Arizona and New Mexico. The Chiricahuas were mostly migratory following the seasons, hunting and farming. When food was scarce, it was the custom to raid neighboring tribes.

Raids and vengeance were an honorable way of life among the tribes of this region. By the time American settlers began arriving in the area, the Spanish had become entrenched in the area. They were always looking for Indian slaves and Christian converts. One of the most pivotal moments in Geronimo's life was in 1858 when he returned home from a trading excursion into Mexico. He found his wife, his mother and his three young children murdered by Spanish troops from Mexico.

This reportedly caused him to have such a hatred of the whites that he vowed to kill as many as he could. From that day on he took every opportunity he could to terrorize Mexican settlements and soon after this incident he received his power, which came to him in visions. Geronimo was never a chief, but a medicine man, a seer and a spiritual and intellectual leader both in and out of battle.

The Apache chiefs depended on his wisdom. When the Chiricahua were forcibly removed (1876) to arid land at San Carlos, in eastern Arizona, Geronimo fled with a band of followers into Mexico. He was soon arrested and returned to the new reservation. For the remainder of the 1870s, he and Juh led a quiet life on the reservation, but with the slaying of an Apache prophet in 1881, they returned to full-time activities from a secret camp in the Sierra Madre Mountains. In 1875 all Apaches west of the Rio Grande were ordered to the San Carlos Reservation.

Geronimo escaped from the reservation three times and although he surrendered, he always managed to avoid capture. In 1876, the U.S. Army tried to move the Chiricahuas onto a reservation, but Geronimo fled to Mexico eluding the troops for over a decade. Sensationalized press reports exaggerated Geronimo's activities, making him the most feared and infamous Apache. The last few months of the campaign required over 5,000 soldiers, one-quarter of the entire Army, and 500 scouts, and perhaps up to 3,000 Mexican soldiers to track down Geronimo and his band.

In May 1882, Apache scouts working for the U.S. army surprised Geronimo in his mountain sanctuary, and he agreed to return with his people to the reservation. After a year of farming, the sudden arrest and imprisonment of the Apache warrior Ka-ya-ten-nae, together with rumors of impending trials and hangings, prompted Geronimo to flee on May 17, 1885, with 35 warriors and 109 women, children and youths. In January 1886, Apache scouts penetrated Juh's seemingly impregnable hideout. This action induced Geronimo to surrender (Mar. 25, 1886) to Gen. George CROOK. Geronimo later fled but finally surrendered to

Gen. Nelson MILES on Sept. 4, 1886. The government breached its agreement and transported Geronimo and nearly 450 Apache men, women, and children to Florida for confinement in Forts Marion and Pickens. In 1894 they were removed to Fort Sill in Oklahoma. Geronimo became a rancher, appeared (1904) at the Louisiana Purchase Exposition in St. Louis, sold Geronimo souvenirs, and rode in President Theodore Roosevelt's 1905 inaugural parade. Geronimo's final surrender in 1886 was the last significant Indian guerrilla action in the United States.

At the end, his group consisted of only 16 warriors, 12 women, and 6 children. Upon their surrender, Geronimo and over 300 of his fellow Chiricahuas were shipped to Fort Marion, Florida. One year later many of them were relocated to the Mt. Vernon barracks in Alabama, where about one quarter died from tuberculosis and other diseases. Geronimo died on Feb. 17, 1909, a prisoner of war, unable to return to his homeland.

Chato was one of Cochise's twelve captains who met General Howard at the Treaty of Dragoon Springs. After the treaty was broken by the politicians, Chato joined the U.S. Army as a scout. He helped to bring his own people to subjugation, always believing the promise that they would be accorded the same rights and treatment as other Americans. Because of his valor he was called to Washington to receive a medal from the President. It was he, Chato, that whirlwind of destructiveness and ferocity, commanding 200 Apache scouts under General Crook who brought the rapacious career of Geronimo to an end.

Of the surrender of Geronimo, General Crook said, "The surrender of Geronimo could not have been effected except for the assistance of Chato and his scouts. For their allegiance, they have been rewarded by captivity in a strange land." Of the medal given him by President Grover Cleveland, Chato said, "Why was I given a medal to wear in the guardhouse?" And that is where Chato spent the next twenty-seven years of his life, for on his return from Washington by train, he was arrested along with all Chiricahuas, by the Army.

He remained a prisoner of the U.S. Army for longer than any prisoner in U.S. Army history. Political policy had changed suddenly in Washington and the bemedaled hero became a prisoner. Coming home one dark, cold night from the town of White Tail, New Mexico, Chato's Model-T ran off the steep mountain road. The eighty year old warrior died in an icy stream. He was mourned throughout Otero County, New Mexico and in the Mescalero Reservation.

As a young man, Naiche (means "the Mischief Maker" or "Meddlesome One") led many raids against white settlers. When his older brother TAZA died of pneumonia in 1876m he became chief of the Chiricahua Apaches. In 1879, Naiche resisted relocation to the San Carlos Apache Reservation and went to Mexico with GERONIMO's Band. While ensconced in the Sierra Madre south of Rio Grande, Naiche and Geronimo attacked American and Mexican communities with relative impunity.

While Naiche was certainly the hereditary chief of the Chiricahua Apaches at this time, it appears that Geronimo was viewed as the great leader and probably persuaded Naiche, the younger man, to submit to his leadership during these campaigns. During the early 180s, the U.S. Army relentlessly tracked the rebellious Chiricahua Apaches until Naiche surrendered on May 25,1883, to General George Crook. For a while, Naiche and Geronimo languished at the San Carlos Reservation, but in 1885, the two leaders left with over one hundred men in a last attempt to avoid American control.

By September 1886, Apache scouts and detachments of the U.S. Army were able to force their surrender in the inhospitable terrain of Mexico. Soon after the Chiricahuas were captured, Naiche and Geronimo and their men were incarcerated first at Fort Marion, Florida, and then at Mount

Vernon Barracks in Alberta. Although Naiche and his men wanted return home to Arizona, angry white settlers there prevented it.

After Kiowa and Comanche leaders invited the Chiricahua Apaches to share their reservation, Naiche and 295 other Apaches relocated to Fort Sill, Oklahoma, on October 4, 1895. Naiche remained in Oklahoma until 1913. He eventually returned to the Southwest, where he lived in peace for eight years, dying of influenza at Mescalero, New Mexico, in 1921.

Victorio was a skilled strategist, known for his bravery. He and his men battled both the Mexicans and the Americans from 1863 to 1877. In 1877 Victorio signed a peace treaty on behalf of the Apache. When the U.S. unilaterally broke the treaty after just four months, Victorio and his men kept on raiding, hiding in the mountains to survive. Over the next couple of years Victorio signed more treaties, was captured, was indicted, and always managed to escape. In 1880 his band was cornered, and in a two-day battle most of them were wiped out. It is unclear whether Victorio was killed in battle or took his own life as the army closed in on him. The Apache and their foes respected and admired Victorio for his bravery and tenacity against incredible odds.

Gouyen

Gouyen, meaning "Wise Woman," was born into Chief Victorio's Warm Springs Apache band around 1880. One day, while the group was resting at Tres Castillos, New Mexico, it was attacked by Mexicans. When the offensive was over, seventy-eight Apaches had been murdered and only seventeen had escaped, including Gouyen and her young son, Kaywaykla. Her baby daughter, however, was murdered and shortly afterwards her husband was killed in a Comanche raid while visiting the Mescalero Apaches.

A legendary tale is told about the revenge of Gouyen. One night following her husband's death, she put on her buckskin puberty ceremony dress and left the camp carrying a water jug, dried meat, and a bone awl and sinew for repairing her moccasins. She was looking for the Comanche chief who had killed her husband. Finally, she found him engaged in a Victory Dance around a bonfire with her husband's scalp hanging from his belt. Gouyen slipped into the circle of dancers, seduced the chief, and killed him, avenging her husband's death. Then she scalped him, cut his beaded breechcloth from his body and tore off his moccasins. She then returned to her camp to present her in-laws with the Comanche leader's scalp, his clothing and his footwear.

Gouyen remarried an Apache warrior named Ka-ya-ten-nae. Later, she and her family were taken prisoner by the U.S. Army and held at Fort Sill, Oklahoma, where she died./

Lozen

Lozen was born into the Chihenne, Warm Springs Apache band, during the late 1840's. She was the sister of Chief Victorio and a skillful warrior, a prophet, and an outstanding medicine woman. Victorio is quoted as saying, "Lozen is my right hand... strong as a man, braver than most, and cunning in strategy, Lozen is a shield to her people."

Legend has it that Lozen was able to use her powers in battle to learn the movements of the enemy and that she helped each band that she accompanied to successfully avoid capture. After Victorio's death, Lozen continued to ride with Chief Nana, and eventually joined forces with Geronimo's band, eluding capture until she finally surrendered with this last group of free Apaches in 1886. She died of tuberculosis at the Mount Vernon Barracks in Mobile, Alabama

White Mountain Apache Tribe is located in the east central region of Arizona, 194 miles northeast of Phoenix. Located on the Apache, Gila and Navajo Counties, the White

Mountain Apaches reside on 1.6 million acres at its ancestral homeland on the Fort Apache Indian Reservation.

On November 9, 1891, by Executive Order the Fort Apache Indian Reservation was established. It is now known as the White Mountain Apache Reservation. It originally included the San Carlos Apache Reservation but was separated by an act of Congress in 1897.

The White Mountain Apache are the direct descendants of the original tribes that lived in this area. The people were once nomadic, however, they now occupy permanent dwellings and depend on livestock, agriculture, tourism and various tribal enterprises for their livelihood.

White Mountain Apaches hold dearly to their traditions—from their strong beliefs, the long free-handing shirt (adopted in 1870), to the Crown Dance and basketry.

The Tribe has over 12,000 members located on nine major reservation communities. Whiteriver, the capital, is the largest community with over 2,500 residents. The topography ranges from 11,000 feet to 3, 000 feet at the Salt River Canyon with its Pre-Cambrian history.

26

Indian Ghost Dance

Ghost dance. A ceremonial religious dance connected with the messiah doctrine, which originated among the Paviotso in Nevada about 1888, and spread rapidly among other tribes until it numbered among its adherents nearly all the Indians of the interior basin, from Missouri river to or beyond the Rockies. The prophet of the religion was a young Paiute Indian, at that time not yet 35 years of age, known among his own people as Wovoka ('Cutter'), and 'commonly called by the whites Jack Wilson, from having worked in the family of a ranchman named Wilson.

Wovoka seems already to have established his reputation as a medicine-man when, about the close of 1888, he was attacked by a dangerous fever. While he was ill an eclipse spread excitement among the Indians, with the result that Wovoka became delirious and imagined that he had been taken into the spirit world, and there received a direct revelation from the God of the Indians.

Briefly stated, the revelation was to the effect that a new dispensation was close at hand by which the Indians would be restored to their inheritance and reunited with their departed friends, and that they must prepare for the event by practicing the songs and dance ceremonies which the prophet gave them.

Within a very short time the dance spread to the tribes east of the mountains, where it became known commonly only as the Spirit or Ghost dance. The dancers, men and women together, held hands, and moved slowly around in a circle, facing toward the center, keeping time to songs that were sung without any instrumental accompaniment. Hypnotic trances were a common feature of the dance.

Among the Sioux in Dakota the excitement, aggravated by local grievances, led to an outbreak in the winter of 1890-91. The principal events in this connection were the killing of Sitting Bull, Dec. 15, 1890, and the massacre at Wounded Knee, Dec. 29.

The doctrine has now faded out, and the dance exists only as an occasional social function. In the Crow dance of the Cheyenne and Arapaho, a later development from the Ghost dance proper, the drum is used, and many of the ordinary tribal dances have incorporated Ghost-dance features, including even the hypnotic trances.

The belief in the coming of a messiah, or deliverer, who shall restore his people to a condition of primitive simplicity and happiness, is probably as universal as the human race, and takes on special emphasis among peoples that have been long subjected to alien domination. In some cases the idea seems to have originated from a myth, but in general it play safely be assumed that it springs from a natural human longing.

Both the Quichua of Peru and the Aztec of Mexico, as well as more cultured races, had elaborate messiah traditions, of which the first Spanish invaders were quick to take advantage, representing themselves as the long-expected restorers of ancient happiness. Within the United States nearly every great tribal movement originated in the teaching of some messianic prophet.

This is notably true of the Pontiac conspiracy in 1763-64, and of the combination organized by Tecumseh and his brother, the prophet Tenskwatawa, shortly before the War of 1812. Of similar nature in more recent times is the doctrine formulated on Columbia river by Smohalla.

Men's Traditional Straight Dances

Men's Traditional/ Straight Dancers serve as storytellers in motion. As they dance, they act out feats of bravery and prowess. The dance records the history of tribal victories in battle and the hunt.

Northern Dancers act out war parties attacking enemies. Notice that they always face the enemy, avoiding turns in a complete circle. Braves may choose to paint their faces to add to their fierceness. On the other hand, Southern Dancers may tell of a hunter tracking an animal or a warrior on the trail of a war party. Moving counterclockwise, dancers may even portray the hunt by imitating animals with side to side head movements.

In Men's Traditional style, dancers wear one bustle of natural turkey, pheasant, or eagle feathers (where legal), in addition to buckskin attire, breastplates, and a headdress of deer or horse hair called a "roach." In contrast, Southern Straight dancers may wear a ribbon shirt, without a bustle, buckskin leggings, and the usual bone breastplate. Southern headdresses may even be made of porcupine with an otter tail extension down the dancer's back. Look for tribal differences in regalia. The dancer's footwork is basically a toe-heel step. Note the harmony of their movements with the drum beat. Try to interpret their motions as they act out stories of valor.

MEN'S TRADITIONAL SNEAK-UP DANCE

The Sneak-Up is an ancient storytelling dance having several origins. In one version, a warrior acts out a battle where the enemy spots him, so he has to begin the attack anew. In the end, he does a victory dance.

Another version involves a hunter tracking a deer. His prey spots him, and he has to try again. The third version enacts a warrior in battle. He searches for a wounded friend, and upon finding him, he brings the friend to safety.

Only men perform the Sneak-Up Dance, as it was a way to teach young boys how to surprise prey or an enemy. Notice that when the drum beats fast, dancers lower themselves closer to the ground to hide, and then survey the area, checking for potential dangers.

Hoop Dance

Several tribes boast gifted dancers who are able to complete a dance form of storytelling with hoops. The dancer picks up one hoop at a time, and then increases, each hoop completing a new symbol of nature. The dance is a real feat of coordination, as the dancer must maintain his movements to the beat of the drum at all times!

WOMEN'S TRADITIONAL & STRAIGHT DANCES

Originating with Northern tribes, Women's Traditional is now performed by Southern tribes, as well. This dance reflects the importance of women in Indian society in accordance with their roles as givers of life, keepers of home and family, decision - makers, and leaders in the Indian community. Northern Style dancers remain in one position or area, lightly bouncing to the drum beats.

However, Southern Style dancers move in clockwise circles, stepping to a slightly slower rhythm. The two styles are in sharp contrast, often necessitating that the Women's Northern and Southern Traditional be danced as two separate events.

During "honor beats" of the drum, women dancers salute the drum with their fans, referred to as "catching the spirit of the drum."

Women's Traditional Straight dancers wear buckskin or cloth dresses with matching leggings and purses, beaded moccasins, and necklaces or bone breastplates. Feathers and beadwork are worn in the hair. A folded shawl over the left arm completes the regalia, as the long fringes sway in harmony with their steps to the beat of the drum.

Watch for the graceful swaying movements as the dancers dip, sway, and step with an air of regal dignity.

MEN'S FANCY (WAR) DANCE

The Fancy War Dance took on new significance after the last Indian Wars as a tradition recalling pride and culture for the next generation. After World War II, Men's Traditional dance and dress styles became increasingly more fancy, accented by elaborate beadwork and colored feather bustles.

Men's Fancy Dancers use intricate steps to the fast beats of the drum. They twirl, turn, step, and pose. Audiences can feel the excitement generated by their fast movements. Perhaps no other dance captures the individual style of each warrior dancer. The fast pace requires real stamina.

Today's Fancy Dancers wear two feather bustles, a smaller one at the back of the neck, a larger at the back of the waist. Foot and leg movements are more elevated, and visual elements in costume, paint, materials, and colors are meant to attract attention. Elaborate regalia may include roach headdress with feathers on "rockers," two colorful feather bustles, sheep skin below the knees with bells attached, ribbon shirts, and matching breechcloths. Footwear is ever changing; some prefer traditional beaded moccasins, while others add beadwork to dance sneakers or water shoes to allow flexibility of footwork. Note their high stepping motions, as well as chest and head movements.

Women's Fancy Dance

Women's Fancy Dancing, a relatively new dance style, is more vigorous than other women's dance styles and similar to Men's Fancy Dancing. Quickly adopted by all tribes, each dancer has her own unique style. Footwork is more intricate and fast paced. High steps are a part of the motion of the dancer as she twirls and bounces freely. Fully outfitted Women's Fancy Dancers wear cloth dresses of colorful material, beaded moccasins and leggings, a single plume in the hair, and a coordinating fancy shawl tucked under a cape at the shoulders.

Watch the dancer as she uses her shawl and shoulders to create fluid motions while keeping her footwork in harmony with the fast paced drum rhythm.

Men's Grass Dance

Perhaps the oldest of all tribal dances, the Grass Dance allows the dancer to use his whole body to create free flowing movements to a slower drumbeat. Some say the dance is merely an expression of the swaying movements of tall prairie grass on a windy day. The most popular account recollects the purpose of the Grass Dance as stomping down the prairie grass to prepare grounds for ceremonies. Watch the Grass Dancer, clad in colorful yarn regalia, as he sways his lower body, legs, and feet in an ancient, abstract style.

WOMEN'S JINGLE

Dress Dance

Originating from the Great Lakes and Canadian tribes, women's movements in the Jingle Dance are more confined. The tight-fitting, colorful cloth dress only allows a dancer to move her feet up, down, back, and forth to the drum beat. Hands are placed at the hips.

A dancer's full emphasis is put into shaking the long, tubular cones sewn in rows covering the dress. According to legend, each dress took one year and one day to make. Every day one jingle was added along with a prayer. When the dress was finally finished, it had 366 cones and was appreciated by the owner for the time, effort, prayers, and personality of the dress. Made from soup or snuff can tops, the cones form a "fringe-like" decoration. Listen to the jingles accompany the drum beat.

Nanticoke Toe Dance

Elders of our tribe, such as E. Patience Harmon, remembered only one traditional Nanticoke women's dance. The music is one of two songs she recollected from earlier Nanticoke Powwows held at Thanksgiving during the 1930's - '40's. We do this dance to honor the Elders. Look closely because the ladies never allow their heels to touch the ground as they gracefully dance and turn.

NATIVE AMERICAN SOCIAL DANCES

Two Step and Rabbit Dances

Long ago, when Indian Nations met at council fires, social dances for couples followed. The Two Step is a general dance where visitors are welcome. Two lead dancers, as a couple, guide other pairs of male and female dancers who follow them around the dance area.

Traditionally, the Two Step and Rabbit Dances are "ladies choice" dances where women ask the men to dance. In more traditional times, if a man refused a woman's dance request, he would pay restitution for the insult. In modern times, some emcees will set a restitution fee of five dollars.

Either way, a man's refusal was considered bad luck.According to the legend of the Rabbit Dance, a man's refusal could cause him to turn into a rabbit!

The simple steps and bouncing motions make it a popular and fun social dance. Notice that the couples join hands, arm over arm, and step side-by-side around the dance circle to the lively beat of the dance.

Crow Hop

The Crow Hop originated from Western Tribes. It, too, is a social dance meant to mimic the crow as he bounces around the field. One legend states that the crow brought fire to our land to keep our ancestors alive through the cold winter. Dancers imitate bird-like movements, hopping sideto-side, first on one foot and then on the other.

Shake Dance

Also a Western tribal dance, the Shake Dance is another fun social dance. The drum imitates a "shaking" sound, while the dancers imitate the movements of the prairie chicken. Watch as the dancers "fluff their feathers" to "shake off the sand."

Snake Dance

Algonquian Woodland tribes profess that the Snake Dance tells the story of life. Dancers demonstrate the life cycle of a snake, from the time its life begins, through the next four stages of its life cycle, until its final stage of entering the Spirit World. Look at the dancers join hands and follow the lead dancers, moving rhythmically in snake-like motions.

Round Dance

Easily considered the most popular of the social dances, the Round Dance is a circle dance derived from earlier tribal Friendship Dances. Today, it is performed as an "open" Friendship Dance in which everyone, including visitors, may participate, whether in powwow dress or plain clothes.

The Round Dance is usually performed near the end of each dance session. Be sure to join us in the dance area as we clasp hands in friendship to form several large circles representing all people of the Earth.

NATIVE AMERICAN SPECIALTY DANCES

Ribbon Dance

The Ribbon Dance is one of the Specialty Dances performed at powwows. It is beautiful, in part because of the long, colorful ribbons which are intertwined throughout the dance. More importantly, the dance portrays the Native American wedding ceremony.

The dance begins with three couples. Each of the women carries a different colored ribbon. The first woman carries a red ribbon which represents the men of the tribe. The second woman holds a blue ribbon which symbolizes the women of the tribe. The third woman carries a yellow ribbon representing the Great Spirit. When the drum starts, the three couples separate into different directions, only to meet together at the center of the dance circle.

The men face the women and take one end of their partners' ribbon. Then, the men braid the three ribbons together to symbolize the coming together of a man and a woman with the blessing of the Great Spirit. The ribbons are then unbraided and encircled about the waists of the women. The women must unwrap themselves, turning to each of the four directions of the world - north, east, south, and west. Finally, the men return the ribbons to the women, the couples separate, and they dance their way out of the circle.

Spear and Shield Dance

As two male warriors enter the dance circle, they face one another to measure each other's courage. They separate to stalk and challenge. A shield is used to thwart attacks from the spear of the opponent. This is a battle to the death, and only one warrior will survive. The best warrior does a final dance to honor his opponent's courage and to celebrate his victory.

Shawl Dance

Performed by the women of the tribe, the ladies display shawls representing the winged creatures of the Earth. Birds are an honored part of our past; not just for food, but for the feathers so important to our culture. Symbolically, birds were considered as the winged creatures closest to the

Great Spirit in Heaven. Also, birds traveled the four corners of the Earth.

The dance begins as a line of women, wrapped in shawls, enters the dance circle. The women appear to "fly"using their shawls as "wings." They stop and face the four sacred directions, to show respect for the "Four Faces of the Earth." Weaving in and around each other at each stop, they finally come together in a circle. When the drum stops, the dancers "ruffle their feathers" with the fringe on the shawls, & exit to the drum beat.

27

The Change and Retention of the Tribal Art & Cultural Heritage in Indian Subcontinent

India has 90 millions of tribal population of different Community groups. The neighboring countries Bangladesh, Bhutan and Nepal have also considerable number of tribal community groups having significant population. It is believed that most of the tribal communities live in neighboring countries have migrated from Indian provincial states Jharkhand, Chhattishgarh, West Bengal, Bihar Assam and Orissa. In these provincial states of India the tribal concentration is overwhelming. The major and notable tribes are Santhal, Oraon, Munda, Kharia, Ho.

These communities have migrated to Bangladesh, Nepal, and Bhuttan during the British regime in the centuries ago as labourer to work in the tea garden and other works. Within India also these tribes have migrated from one state to other in considerable number in search of livelihood and settled in the respective areas.

The tribal Art and Cultural Heritage, which has an unique feature and has glorious past have under gone some changes due to migration, cultural contacts, industrialization, urbanization, changing economic scenario, westernization globalization etc. These factors of change have resulted the questions of retention of their age old art and cultural heritage and also the different aspects of folk life, culture and traditions, the tribal art which is widely accepted as full of rich artistic expression and aesthetic emotion has now been facing threat of extinction to some extent.

Oral tradition, oral literature, religion, linguistic panaroma which have divergent look but at the same time the syncretism and congregation of various aspects of tribal life, norms, customs, have been taking place. Due to globalization and economic liberalization their traditional system economic activities, intellectual property right have been threatened. Parodoxy, situation of change & continuity of the tribal Art and cultural system in the folk life & tradition should be carefully examined by anthropologists, social scientists and ethnographers. This panel will consist 3 -4 papers which will cover different aspects of tribal life.

About forty different ethnic tribal races reside in different states of Eastern India i.e. Jharkhand, Bihar, Orissa, West - Bengal and Manipur. The main tribal races are Oraon, Munda, Santhal, Kharia, Bhumij, Ho, Rabha, Toto, Lodha, Mench etc. The tribal communities are basically nature loving and resides mostly in forests or adjoining to forests with peace, security and harmony, maintaining their rich socio-cultural heritage since time immemorial.

This mass is also known as Forest Dependent Population, as they depends on forest flora and Fauna for their subsistence and livelihood. There has been continuous attack on the Socio-cultural heritage as well as Economic Institutions of this population, with the emergence of the so called different modern developmental projects in the name of industrialization, urbanization, mining (specially open cast mining), deforestation and desertification and many others.

All these projects with the concept of Globalization and Patent Laws has been continuously Hampering the Pre-historic rich socio-cultural heritage and the socio-economic institutions of different tribal communities, by making them displaced from their original Hamlets and are being compelled to shift to the urban area for their subsistence and livelihood, leaving behind their pre-historic socio-cultural heritage and the economic institutions.

The new changed habitat is not conducive for them at all and are put to CROSS-ROAD. The tribal communities are even not in a position to adjust in the new urban culture. All these developmental projects has proved to be innihilator for the indigenous mass in general and the tribal communities in particular. This is becoming a burning problem and giving direct threat even to the existence of the tribal communities in the states of Eastern India. If this trend remains unabated there is every possibility of the vanishing of the tribal communities and finally their rich pre-historical socio-cultural heritage too will be demolished.

The demographic data of the tribal communities for the past 30-40 years also clearly shows continuous reduction in their population. At last this can be concluded with a line that this needs an national level debate and opinions of social scientists, bio-scientists, social think tanks, economists and political analysis should be invited & procured to get a permanent solution to it. The situation can be controlled by giving proper recognition and participation of the indigenous people (both tribes & non tribes) in different developmental projects. The developmental model should be pro-tribal, pro - indigenous and pro-environment preservation.

The models should be framed keeping in mind the preservation of indigenous rights of the indigenous mass, tribes and the non-tribes. The full paper will highlight the problem in a very logical scientific manner as how the socio-cultural heritage and socio-economic institutions of the indigenous people in general & the tribes in particular are being brought to cross road with some concrete suggestions.

Folk traditions have significant importance in the Indian society. The folk traditions are recognized as the socio-cultural image of the human society. Each one of the races has own folk traditions. The newly formed Jharkhand state of the Indian republic is universally known not only for it's forests and mineral wealth but also for it's rich Tribal and non-tribal socio - cultural heritages.

Thirty - two different tribal communities resides in different areas of Jharkhand state in natural habitats since pre-historic period with peace and harmony maintaining their rich socio-cultural heritage. Chhau - dance is one of the most important and popular folk dances among the indigenous population (both tribes and non - tribes) of Jharkhand state. Chhau dance is also popular in different districts of adjoining states, i.e. West - Bengal, Orissa and Chattisgarh. Chhau - dance is based on folk tales related to nature, with no trace in the Holy Sculptures and Historical Sculptures.

According to folk tales the origin of Chhau - dance is traced from the Kaling's victory by King Ashoka. During their return after victory the soldiers while staying in the forests of Singhbhum district under Jharkhand state performed group dances putting Masks. This mask wearing group dance of the soldiers was adopted by the Tribals of Sinbhum district and this gave the birth of present Chhau - dance or Paika dance, which became very popular among the tribes. Paika literally means soldier.

Contributions of Chhau-dance Gurus namely Shri Kedar Nath Sahu, Sri Nepal Mahto and Sri Gambhir Singh to the enrichment of Chhau - dance cannot be forgotten, who has bought Chhau-dance not only on the National level but also on International scenario by stage presentations in different countries like U.S.A., Europe, Italy, France, Germany, England, Russia, Singapur, Japan and others. This has certainly been proved to strengthen brotherhood and cultural relations at International level.

Guru Kedar Nath and Guru Nepal Mahto have been honoured with "Padma Shree" by the Government of India on the recognition of their contributions to the Chhau - dance. Chhau-dance is getting momentum day by day and it needs further assistance from Government machinery so that this historical tribal cultural heritage could not be vanished.

Certain training centers of tribal folk dances are being managed in Singhbhum and Saraikela districts of Jharkhand, Mayurbhanj & Rairangpur of Orissa and Purulia district of West Bengal state.The dance and songs related to Chhau - dance are the major activities in the villages and towns of Jharkhand particularly during summer season. Chhau dance fairs are organized in every village in a massive way. People congregate in these fairs in thousands and actively take part without any discrimination on caste and creed. Tribals & non-tribals, Christians, Muslims, men & women, old & young all actively participate in these occasions. It can be concluded that Chhau-dance festivals provide opportunities for free social relations above caste and creed and it promotes brotherhood tolerance and solidarity.

Though, the Jharkhand has its new entity as one of the state of India which is carved out of Bihar in 2000, but the 'Jharkhand culture ' has a greater connotation, culturally and geographically, which extends to some parts of West Bengal, Orissa and Chattisgarh. Jharkhand is one of the richest cultural regions in the country. This is the only place in the country where the three major culture components i.e. Austric, Dravidian and the Aryan, have created a cultural synthesis of a unique kind.

All layers of civilization from hunting - gathering culture to the industrial culture are evidenced in this area. Jharkhand has a rich culture heritage of tribal people. They have unique arts and culture in consonance with their surroundings, which reflect in the activities of their life. Arts and culture are the part of their daily activities. When they move, they dance and when they speak they sing. These movements vary from ethnic group to ethnic group.

Here, in this paper, an attempt has been made to look into the performing arts of the tribes of Jharkhand. The performing arts are the music and dances. The music and dances are in many way unique in nature. In its simplest and most obvious from and meaning, a performing art is an art which lives only when it is being performed like, music, dance or the theatre.

In Jharkhand the popular dances are the Chhau dance, Natua dance, Nachni dance etc., besides many festival dances which reflect their agricultural activities. The Chhau and Natua are very fast dance with aerobatic expressions. The Chhau dance has acquired national and International fame, and has been performed at different places. Chhau dance has some local variations and in Jharkhand, it has grouped into three schools, such as Manbhum, Mayurbhanj and Saraikela school of Chhau. The Chhau artists use masks during their performances.

Bibliography

Abhinaya-Candrika and Odissidance: *Sushma Kulshreshtha and A.C. Sarangi, Eastern Book Linkers,* Delhi 2001

Adavus and Sancharis in Bharatanatyam: *Vidya Bhavani Suresh, Skanda Pub.,* Chennai, 2002

Ang Kavya : Nomenclature for Hand Movements and Feet Positions in Kathak: *Pt. Birju Maharaj, Har-Anand,* New Delhi, 2002

Ashish Khokar's Attendance : The Dance Annual of India: *Shanta Serbjeet Singh, Ekah-Printways,* New Delhi, 2003-04

Bhaava Niroopanna/Kanak Rele: *Nalanda Dance Research Centre,* Mumbai, 1996

Bharatanatyam: *Ashish Mohan Khokar, Rupa & Co.,* New Delhi, 2002

Bharata Natyam : Du Temple a La Scene: *Raghunath Manet, Tala Sruti,* Pondicherry, 1999

Bharatanatyam : How to...: *Jayalakshmi Eshwar., B.R. Pub.,* Delhi, 2002

Chidambaram Home of Nataraja: *Vivek Nanda with George Michell,* New Delhi, 2004

Dance Dialects of India: *Ragini Devi, Motilal Banarsidass,* Delhi, 2002

Dhananjayan on Indian Classical Dance: *V.P. Dhananjayan, B.R. Rhythms,* Delhi, 2004

Kathak Sagar: *Bharti Gupta, Radha Pub.,* New Delhi, 2004

Nangiar Koothu : The Classical Dance-Theatre of the Nangiar-s: *Nirmala Paniker, Natana Kairali,* Trichur, 1992

Rukmini Devi Arundale : Birth Centenary Volume: *Shakuntala Ramani, Kalakshetra Foundation,* Chennai, 2003

Rukmini Devi : Bharata Natya: *Kalakshetra Pub.,* Chennai, 2003

The Science of Bharata Natyam: *Saroja Vaidyanathan, Kanishka,* Delhi, 2000

Staging Resistance Plays by Women in Translation: *Tutun Mukherjee, Oxford University Press,* New Delhi, 2005

Index

□□□